AMERICAN LITERATURE LIFE FROM MODERN TO POSTMODERN 1946–PRESENT

CONTENTS

Author: **Krista L. White, B.S.**

Editor: Alan Christopherson, M.S.

Graphic Design: Lauren Durain, A.S.T.

Alpha Omega Publications®

804 N. 2nd Ave. E., Rock Rapids, IA 51246-1759
© MM by Alpha Omega Publications, Inc. All rights reserved.
LIFEPAC is a registered trademark of Alpha Omega Publications, Inc.

"The Displaced Person" by Flannery O'Connor, from *The Complete Stories of Flannery O'Connor*. © 1971 by the Estate of Flannery O'Connor used by permission of Farrar, Straus, and Giroux, Inc.

"Root Cellar", © 1943 by Modern Poetry Association, Inc. from THE COLLECTED POEMS OF THEODORE ROETHKE by Theodore Roethke. Used by permission of Doubleday, a division of Random House, Inc.

"A Worn Path" From A CURTAIN OF GREEN AND OTHER STORIES, © 1941 and renewed by Eudora Welty, reprinted by permission of Harcourt, Inc.

"Separating" From PROBLEMS AND OTHER STORIES by John Updike. Reprinted by permission of Alfred A. Knopf, a Division of Random House, Inc.

"Epilogue" From DAY BY DAY by Robert Lowell. © 1977 by Robert Lowell. Reprinted by permission of Farrar, Straus, and Giroux, LLC.

"Prologue" From INVISIBLE MAN by Ralph Ellison. © 1952 by Ralph Ellison. Reprinted by permission of Random House, Inc.

"The Lovers of the Poor" by Gwendolyn Brooks. © Third World Press. Reprinted by permission of Third World Press.

Alpha Omega Publications, Inc.

804 N. 2nd Ave. E., Rock Rapids, IA 51246-1759

AMERICAN LITERATURE LIFEPAC 5
1946 – PRESENT

OBJECTIVES:

1. Gain an overview of the rise and fall of the modern era.
2. Discern the prevalent ideas that led to the beginning of postmodernism.
3. Evaluate the philosophical undercurrents of postmodernism in relation to biblical Christianity.
4. Recognize the dominant themes and techniques used in literature at the end of the twentieth century.

VOCABULARY:

absolute truth - truth that is not subject to change; it is always true
authenticate - to establish as accurate or reliable
disillusion - to free from unrealistic or romantic views
divergent - moving in different directions from a common point
empirical - depending upon experience or experimentation
existentialism - the belief that man creates his own meaning and course of life through the choices he makes
ideology - the body of beliefs of a society or social movement
myriad - an infinitely large number; countless or innumerable
objective - free from individual opinions; based upon fact; unbiased
permissive - allowing behavior that is otherwise forbidden
regiment - to organize for the purpose of control
relativism - any theory that changes with the shifting ideals of individuals and their environment

I. THE BIRTH OF POSTMODERNISM
INTRODUCTION

Tower of Babel. Genesis 11 records the history of the Tower of Babel. At that time, the whole world spoke one language and was unified in its ideology and purpose. The people, proud of their great technological advances, decided that they no longer needed God. By the sheer might of their own abilities, they proposed to "remake" society, building it on their own laws rather than on the law of God. They said, "'Come, let us build ourselves a city, with a tower that reaches to the heavens, so that we may make a name for ourselves'" (Gen. 11:4).

Social critics have observed that the rise of modern society in American follows a similar plot line. A people who were proud of their automobiles, their computers, their moon landings, their weapons of mass destruction, and their scientific methods of birth control, devised to build themselves a city. It would be based on man-made laws, and it would serve to exalt the ways of man rather than the ways of God. Human reason, not divine revelation, would bring the people into a heaven made on earth.

The rise and fall of the Tower of Babel and modernism are similar. As with the Tower of Babel, the building of modernism stopped with the scattering of the peoples. In the confusion over who or what would replace the authority of God, a popular saying emerged: "What is true for you is not necessarily true for me." Society, lacking a cohesive set of absolutes, broke apart, splintering into a myriad of divergent communities. Women opposed men; children opposed their parents; whites opposed minorities; heterosexuals opposed homosexuals; "Pro-lifers" opposed "Pro-choicers"; the Religious Right opposed the Liberal Left; etc.

As we pass from modernism to postmodernism, society is becoming more obsessed with the "right" to choose according to individual ideas of right and wrong. People no longer look to or acknowledge an objective, universal standard of truth. Everyone is doing "what is right in his own eyes" (Judges 17:6). American literature reflects this shift. It, too, has fallen into a downward spiral, beginning with God-oriented, historical accounts during the colonial period; slipping to Romanticized portrayals of nature and man in the nineteenth century; and finally, dropping to man-centered pictures of reality that have only caused disillusionment and confusion.

In the dawning of the postmodern age, the walls of certainty and truth have crumbled and art has tumbled into the gulf of meaninglessness. The only writers and artists worthy of serious attention are those that have not only recorded the fall of truth but also attempted to put the pieces back together again.

Fill in each of the blanks using items from the following word list.

technological	similar	truth
society	human reason	

1.1   The people at the time of the Tower of Babel were proud of their _____ advances.

1.2   Modern society hoped to establish a heaven made on earth that was based on

_____ .

1.3   The rise and fall of the Tower of Babel and modernism are _____ .

1.4   In postmodern society, an objective, universal standard of _____ no longer exists.

1.5   American literature reflects the shifts in _____ .

The Modern Age. Thomas Oden, professor of theology at Drew University, argues that the modern age lasted exactly two hundred years—from 1789 to 1989. At its beginning was the French Revolution, which exalted human reason. In the Cathedral of Notre Dome, the revolutionaries tore down images of Christ and erected a statue of the goddess of Reason. The Rights of Man became superior to the rights of God. Man was enthroned as the ultimate authority. Man and his intellectual abilities would bring society into a state of peace and happiness.

This exaltation of the Rights of Man spread across the globe. In most European countries, democratic states took the place of monarchal systems of government. The people, not a divinely appointed king, ruled the land. In other European countries, the exaltation of human reason manifested itself in the form of socialism and communism.

The Russian Revolution put into practice the economic theories of Karl Marx, instituting a communist state. Marx, borrowing from the scientific theories of Charles Darwin, believed that the lower classes would eventually emerge to the top. This would complete the evolution of society. There would be no upper class or lower class; everyone would be equal. Gene Veith correctly stated, "Communism was the most thoroughgoing attempt to remake society by means of human reason." Devoid of the influence of the Scriptures, it based its advancement on science and human reason.

The appeal of Marxism was deceptive. While claiming to create a utopian state based solely on human reason, it found its power in "oppression and brute force." After World War II, the term *Iron Curtain* came to be used for the barrier against communication and travel that the Communists erected. It limited the citizens of communist states from relations with Western Europe and the United States. Human reason did not lead the people to greater freedom. On the contrary, it led to the greatest horrors that this world has known, namely, the extermination of more than six million Jews in Nazi Germany and the execution and starvation of millions of "class enemies" first in Stalin's Russia and later in China under communist dictator Mao Tse-tung. In 1989, the Berlin Wall was torn down, signaling the fall of the Iron Curtain and the death of the modern age.

In American, the Rights of Man never became as thoroughgoing as in Russia. The Christian roots and capitalistic economy of America were too well grounded in the nation's demeanor. "One nation under God" was not merely a decorative slogan printed on the tokens of free enterprise. The existence of a personal God was and still is recognized by a majority of Americans.

Nevertheless, the Rights of Man did affect American society and culture. From religion to politics, the "right to choose" has been an ever-increasing theme. Thomas Paine was an extremely influential author during the American Revolution. His books *The Rights of Man* and *The Age of Reason* played an enormous part in the French Revolution. He championed the ideas of the Enlightenment, proclaiming, "My mind is my own church." Man was the ultimate authority. The Word of God was nothing more to him than a myth. Paine was a deist who believed that God neither interacted with his Creation nor was concerned about its inhabitants. The world was nothing more than a mechanical instrument. Man was left alone to contend with the impersonal laws of nature. Reason alone could tell a person what was right and what was wrong.

During the 1800s, Romanticism reacted against the cold, impersonal world of deism. Writers such as Emerson and Thornton exalted the virtues of Nature, calling on society to remake itself in Nature's image. Man was looked upon as an innocent victim of the "evil" institutions in society. But Nature could not provide definite answers. Man needed to look to his own choices for the answers to peace and happiness. Once again, the authority of God was dismissed. In the absence of a universal standard of truth, confusion over morals began to affect society. Consequently, poets such as Walt Whitman began to gain a "respectable" place in American literature.

Darwin's *Origin of the Species* brought an end to the Romantic dream. People were not innocent victims living in an evil society. They were animals, willing to kill to survive. The atrocities of the Civil War, World War I, and World War II seemed only to hammer home this point to many people. Science seemed to be able to explain everything. Man was nothing more than flesh and blood. He had no soul. His thoughts were merely the results of chemical reactions in his brain.

This materialistic view of the world drained life of any collective meaning. Artists and writers during the 1920s and 1930s struggled to find order in the apparent chaos. Men such as Ezra Pound looked for meaning in fascism, a government led by a dictator. Others searched for meaning in art. And still others, such as T. S. Eliot and W. H. Auden, returned to orthodox Christianity for truth.

The Modern age was a search for truth apart from Christianity. It was an objective search that based its claims on empirical data. Empirical data are facts derived from experience or experimentation alone. But, as the advocates of modernism found, empirical data cannot answer the "whys" of existence. Life has to have a purpose.

 Underline the correct answer for each of the following statements.

1.6   The (medieval, modern, postmodern) age began with the French Revolution.

1.7   The French Revolution exalted (human reason, divine revelation, the Bible).

1.8   (Communism, Capitalism, Democracy) is the most thoroughgoing attempt to remake society by means of human reason.

1.9   Marxism finds its power in (oppression and brute force, kindness and humility, morals and religion).

1.10   The Iron Curtain limited the citizens of (democratic, communist, socialist) states from relations with Western Europe and the United States.

1.11   (Ezra Pound, T. S. Eliot, Thomas Paine) was an influential author during the American Revolution.

1.12   Thomas Paine believed that (Scripture, human reason, the Constitution) could tell man what was right and what was wrong.

1.13   Emerson and Thoreau called society to remake itself in the image of (nature, heaven, God).

1.14   Darwin theorized that humans were nothing more than (animals, pigs, angels).

1.15   The Modern Age searched for truth apart from (Christianity, communism, Marxism).

The Fifties. The decade following World War II was an era of American bliss. Called the "tranquilized fifties," it was characterized by economic success, technological advances, and social stability. Lives were "ordinary." Husbands earned reasonable wages. Housewives enjoyed their "revolutionary" washers and dryers, automatic coffeepots, electric irons, and vacuum cleaners. Children were taught to say the pledge of allegiance and to obey their parents. In the evenings, the family gathered around the television to watch their favorite programs.

The 1950s were also the beginning of the Space Age. Scientists in the Soviet Union and the United States raced to develop weapons and rocket ships that would go farther and faster. Americans watched on television as the world of fantasy came true. Men placed in little capsules were shot high up into the air, orbited the earth, and then returned home to safety. Science had yet again defied traditional concepts of reality. The human mind and what it could invent seemed to have no boundaries. Like the Tower of Babel, science offered mankind a stairway to heaven. People came to trust technology without reservation.

As a new technology, television had a profound effect on the American public's idea of reality. It brought the world into the living rooms of America. Monumental events happened right before the viewer's eyes. Rather than just reading about it or hearing it later, he or she could watch it happen. Television left no room to question the "truth" of the event. In the technological age, it became the great authenticator of truth— "If it is on television, then it must be true."

From all appearances, it seemed as if the modern age would fulfill its promises of peace and happiness, but all was not well. Underlying the tranquil, orderly surface of the 1950s were mounting problems. Blacks and other minorities still did not have the same rights and privileges as white Americans. The "cold war" with the Soviet Union threatened the nation with instant annihilation. Rock-n-roll, with its wild beat and suggestive dancing, excited teenagers and distressed parents. The modern world was too closed and regimented. It failed to produce meaning beyond the material.

"Letting (Truth) Go." The 1960s erupted with a desire to break with "square" modes of life. In reaction to their parents' materialism and the need for meaning, young people became "flower children." They lived permissive lives filled with "drugs, sex, and rock-n-roll." The period had a profound effect on the following decades. It not only encouraged a rapid decline in morals but also rejected truth. People were told to "let go" and to feel rather than to think. Emotions were allowed to rule, and morality became nothing more than a matter of choice. Many people adopted as their motto, "If it feels good, do it."

In 1961 John F. Kennedy was elected president. He was the youngest president in history and the first Catholic resident of the White House. His connection with the youth and his political association with black leaders brought hope for further "liberation" from the past decade. But his assassination in 1963, coupled with the assassination of Martin Luther King in 1968, brought a crushing revelation to a generation that had not lived through a world war. Hopes and dreams were sometimes killed in cold blood. The expanding military conflict in Vietnam only amplified the disillusionment with the modern age and its talk of objective truth.

For many people who did not understand that God "works all things after the counsel of His will," it was difficult to believe that God existed. "If God is so loving and so powerful, then how could such horrific evil exist?" they asked. "Why do bad things happen to good people?"

Their questions were valid. Unfortunately, Christians armed with the truths of God's sovereignty and the sinfulness of man were ignored. God and objective truth were removed from popular culture. Feelings and pleasure began to guide in the area of religion. People began to seek out New Age cults and religions that made them feel good about themselves. As Gene Veith has outlined, modernism was exchanged for a new world view: "The intellect was replaced by the will. Reason was replaced by emotion. Morality was replaced by relativism. Reality itself became a social construct."

A Rejection of Truth. From intellectuals in the universities to the housewife with three kids, people began to adopt an existential view of life. Existentialism is the "belief that people have absolute freedom of choice." In the absence of objective truth, people believed that there was no meaning to life aside from the one that each individual created. The freedom to choose became important because it allowed one to invent his own reality, his own truths. According to this line of thought, abortion is a *moral* option simply because it is a *legal* option. Simply possessing the "right" to have an abortion removes the act from the realm of right or wrong.

This sort of thinking rests on the popular idea that "there are no absolutes." An absolute truth does not change according to popular opinion. It is always true. To proclaim that there are no absolutes is itself a contradiction in terms. One cannot absolutely dismiss absolute truth without declaring an absolute truth. In other words, to say that "there are no absolutes" is to proclaim an absolute. It is a contradiction that cannot exist.

The often confused and fragmented thought that results from existentialism is typical of the postmodern age. Existentialism itself is directly opposed to Christian thought. It presents choices in areas where the Bible declares that there are none.

The Bible declares that reality or the universe was created by the mind of God and is ruled by Him. Reality is not something that a person can "choose" to create. "For by Him all things were created that are in heaven and that are on the earth, visible and invisible, whether thrones or dominions or principalities or powers. All things were created through Him and for Him" (Colossians 1:16). The Bible also declares that truth is grounded in God. We cannot decide what is "true" according to personal preferences. Jesus contradicted the postmodern notion of "personal truths" when He said, "I am the way, the truth, and the life" (John 14:6). Therefore, there *is* an objective, universal standard of truth and goodness: it is found in God. And, that standard is communicated to us in His Word. The Ten Commandments are a reflection of God's "perfect and moral character."

 Underline the correct answer for each of the following statements.

1.16 The (1930s, 1920s, 1950s) were characterized by economic success, technological advances, and social stability.

1.17 The 1950s were the beginning of the (modern, Space, religious) Age.

1.18 During the 1950s, people came to trust (religion, society, technology) without reservation.

1.19 In the technological age, the (television, Bible, reason of man) became the great authenticator of truth.

1.20 The (1950s, 1960s, 1990s) encouraged a rapid decline in morals and the rejection of absolute truth.

1.21 The election of (Richard Nixon, Gerald Ford, John F. Kennedy) brought hope for further "liberation."

1.22 After the 60s, God and objective truth were removed from (Christian, African-American, popular) culture.

1.23 (Christianity, Marxism, Existentialism) is the belief that people have absolute freedom of choice.

1.24 An absolute truth is (always, sometimes, occasionally) true.

1.25 Existentialism is directly opposed to (Marxist, democratic, Christian) thought.

1.26 (God, Man, Government) alone is the author of truth.

1.27 Reality rests in the mind of (the individual, God, philosophers).

The "Art" of Meaninglessness. Sir Arnold Toynbee, a historian of world civilizations, has observed that societies that stop believing in a universal standard of morals tend to lose their ability to create great pieces of art. As we survey the landscape of American literature, we can see this occurring. Anne Bradstreet, Edward Taylor, and Jonathan Edwards all spoke with beauty about the God who rules over His creation. Nathaniel Hawthorne and Herman Melville argued with the same God, yet with eloquence, acknowledging His presence. Emerson, Thoreau, and Whitman all denounced the God of the Bible and questioned the idea of truth. Their work, though inventive, lacked a connection with the real world. Hemingway and Fitzgerald could paint a clear picture of problems but they left readers without an answer. Their works lack the goodness of wisdom that makes art truly beautiful.

As American culture has transformed, it has moved farther and farther from the deep truths of God. Consequently, we are left with art museums that are filled with dispassionate paintings of Coke bottles. In the postmodern age, television is looked to as the highest form of art. But not all of the culture searches for truth and meaning between channel 4 and channel 33. Many pieces of literature written after World War II deal with serious issues in a thoughtful manner.

Blurred Realities and Striking Prose. At the end of the twentieth century, novels and short stories show elements of traditional works while attempting new techniques appropriate for the era. The blending of nonfiction and fiction reflect a blurred sense of reality. The postmodern era has no universal standard of truth; consequently it is confused in its understanding of reality. Is reality in the mind of the author or in the actual events? This confusion has been emphasized also in the use of the stream-of-consciousness technique much popularized by Henry James and James Joyce. Ralph Ellison's *Invisible Man* uses this technique to delve deeply into the struggles of a black man in New York City.

Fiction writers from the South have emerged from the confusion of the age with works that are called grotesque. Their works depict striking images of humanity and the world. People are often portrayed as cruel and insensitive.

Many of the Southern writers were women, one of the most talented of whom is Flannery O'Connor. As a Christian writer in an unbelieving age, she agreed with her fellow writers in their ugly and often antiheroic presentation of man. She believed that man was sinful, but, as one critic has observed, she differed with them profoundly in that she found that "the meaning of life is centered in our Redemption by Christ." Her works, though filled with shocking events and grotesque characters, point to the grace of God. Hope can be found in Christ. Commenting on her work as a Christian, she said, "The novelist with Christian concerns will find in modern life distortions which are repugnant to him, and his problems will be to make these appear as distortions to an audience which is used to seeing them as natural; and he may well be forced to take ever more violent means to get his vision across to this hostile audience."

Other writers such as John Updike and Arthur Miller have questioned the materialism and self-centeredness that pervades the age. Updike's short stories have been appreciated in both academic and popular circles. As a writer with a deep sense of Christian values, he often pointed out that the problems in postmodern society are moral issues in need of a religious solution.

Poetry, a Return to Tradition. Ironically, some of the most popular poetry to emerge from the era is traditional in form. Writers such as Robert Lowell and Theodore Roethke used traditional forms to beautify their words. Roethke instructed his students to imitate the poets of the past, to "write like someone else." He himself had learned discipline and form from Blake and Yeats.

Lowell was a descendant of James Russell Lowell and a distant relative of Amy Lowell. His family was of the New England elite. As a poet, Lowell struggled with his Puritan past and the radical society of which he was a part. His work progressed from the traditional use of rhythm and meter to free verse. In his later years, his poetry focused more on his personal problems than on public events. He was one of the leading poets of the confessional movement in American poetry.

Works of Freedom and Social Change. Black writers also emerged with ever-increasing talent. Their works reflected the growing need for social change. Many of them threw their energies into protest writings whereas others insisted on reviving their people by other means. Ralph Ellison was heavily criticized for his "absence" from the racial revolution. Gwendolyn Brooks, on the other hand, attempted to establish black community and pride. She imitated the poets of the past while integrating their form with the language and rhythm of her own people.

Only the Beginning. The end of the twentieth century marked only the beginning of the postmodern era. The trends and techniques used did not necessarily reveal what the future might hold for American literature. New styles might be invented or a revival of traditional themes might emerge. The classics of the era are yet to be determined. The authors included in this LIFEPAC are a sampling of the thoughtful talent of this era.

Fill in each of the blanks using items from the following word list.

blurred	social	traditional
stream-of-consciousness	grotesque	God
man	morals	poetry
grace		

1.28   Societies that stop believing in a universal standard of _____ tend to lose their ability to create great pieces of art.

1.29   American culture has moved away from the deep truths of _____ .

1.30   Novels and short stories of the postmodern era show elements of _____ works.

1.31   Blending nonfiction and fiction creates a _____ sense of reality.

1.32   The _____ technique continues to be used in postmodern writing.

1.33   Fiction writers from the South have produced works that have been called

_____ .

1.34   Southern writers have often depicted _____ as ugly and antiheroic.

1.35   The works of Flannery O'Connor point to the _____ of God.

1.36   The most popular _____ to emerge during the postmodern era has been written in traditional form.

1.37   The works of black writers reflected a need for _____ change.

Flannery O'Connor (1925–1964). Robert Drake observed, "[Flannery O'Connor's] overriding strategy is always to shock, embarrass, and even outrage rationalist readers." O'Connor was a Christian novelist who understood the era in which she lived. Often called grotesque, her stories paint a realistic picture of man's sinfulness. She does not allow her readers to find the answers to life and death in man; rather, she points them to the grace that can be found only in Christ.

O'Connor was born in Savannah, Georgia. Early in life, she aspired to be a cartoonist. However, she changed her pursuits to follow a more serious undertaking. She studied at Georgia State College for Women and then at the University of Iowa Writer's Workshop. After beginning her first novel, she discovered that she had lupus, a rare blood disease. The same fatal disease had brought about her father's early death.

Flannery O'Connor Cartoon on inside cover of the 1945 Georgia State College for women year book

Despite the crippling effects of the medicine and the threat of an early death, O'Connor continued to write and lecture. During her life, she published two novels, *Wise Blood* (1952) and *The Violent Bear It Away* (1960), and a collection of short stories, *A Good Man Is Hard to Find* (1955). *Everything That Rises Must Converge* (1965) is a collection of short stories that was published soon after her death.

As a Roman Catholic, O'Connor viewed the world from "the standpoint of Christian orthodoxy." At the center of the meaning of life was the redemption that is provided by Christ. She often drew horrific and startling pictures of people. At times, the behavior of her characters can be quite discomforting. But in all, she was trying to prove to her modern readers that man is not able to save himself. By showing us the ugliness of our sin, she leads us to the Savior.

Underline the correct answer in each of the following statements.

1.38   Flannery O'Connor's stories paint a realistic picture of man's (sinfulness, purity, beauty).

1.39   After beginning her first novel, O'Connor discovered that she had a rare and (fatal, harmless, curable) blood disease.

1.40   The medicine that she took had (crippling, comforting, invigorating) effects.

1.41   At the center of the meaning of life was the redemption that is provided by (man, society, Christ).

*   It is acknowledged that there are some terms in the following story that by todays standards are distasteful, but this is the way the author wrote the work.

What to Look For:

Many of O'Connor's characters have been described as grotesque. She painted them thus to shock people into seeing that people are not "good at heart" but are actually sinful and in desperate need of God's grace. As you read, compare the words and actions of the various characters. Who would you call grotesque and why?

The Displaced Person

THE PEACOCK was following Mrs. Shortley up the road to the hill where she meant to stand. Moving one behind the other, they looked like a complete procession. Her arms were folded and as she mounted the prominence, she might have been the giant wife of the countryside, come out at some sign of danger to see what the trouble was. She stood on two tremendous legs, with the grand self-confidence of a mountain, and rose, up narrowing bulges of granite, to two icy blue points of light that pierced forward, surveying everything. She ignored the white afternoon sun which was creeping behind a ragged wall of cloud as if it pretended to be an intruder and cast her gaze down the red clay road that turned off from the highway.

The peacock stopped just behind her, his tail-glittering green-gold and blue in the sunlight-lifted just enough so that it would not touch the ground. It flowed out on either side like a floating train and his head on the long blue reed-like neck was drawn back as if his attention were fixed in the distance on something no one else could see.

Mrs. Shortley was watching a black car turn through the gate from the highway. Over by the toolshed, about fifteen feet away, the two Negroes, Astor and Sulk, had stopped work to watch. They were hidden by a mulberry tree but Mrs. Shortley knew they were there.

Mrs. McIntyre was coming down the steps of her house to meet the car. She had on her largest smile but Mrs. Shortley, even from her distance, could detect a nervous slide in it. These people who were coming were only hired help, like the Shortleys themselves or the Negroes. Yet here was the owner of the place out to welcome them. Here she was, wearing her best clothes and a string of beads, and now bounding forward with her mouth stretched.

The car stopped at the walk just as she did and the priest was the first to get out. He was a long-legged black-suited old man with a white hat on and a collar that he wore backwards, which, Mrs. Shortley knew, was what priests did who wanted to be known as priests. It was this priest who had arranged for these people to come here. He opened the back door of the car and out jumped two children, a boy and a girl, and then, stepping more slowly, a woman in brown, shaped like a peanut. Then the front door opened and out stepped the man, the Displaced Person. He was short and a little sway-backed and wore gold-rimmed spectacles.

Mrs. Shortley's vision narrowed on him and then widened to include the woman and the two children in a group picture. The first thing that struck her as very peculiar was that they looked like other people. Every time she had seen them in her imagination, the image she had got was of the three bears, walking single file, with wooden shoes on like Dutchmen and sailor hats and bright coats with a lot of buttons. But the woman had on a dress she might have worn herself and the children were dressed like anybody from around. The man had on khaki pants and a blue shirt. Suddenly, as Mrs. McIntyre held out her hand to him, he bobbed down from the waist and kissed it.

Mrs. Shortley jerked her own hand up toward her mouth and then after a second brought it down and rubbed it vigorously on her seat. If Mr. Shortley had tried to kiss her hand, Mrs. McIntyre would have knocked him into the middle of next week, but then Mr. Shortley wouldn't have kissed her hand anyway. He didn't have time to mess around.

She looked closer, squinting. The boy was in the center of the group, talking. He was supposed to speak the most English because he had learned some in Poland

and so he was to listen to his father's Polish and say it in English and then listen to Mrs. McIntyre's English and –say that in Polish. The priest had told Mrs. McIntyre his name was Rudolph and he was twelve and the girl's name was Sledgewig and she was nine. Sledgewig sounded to Mrs. Shortley like something you would name a bug, or vice versa, as if you named a boy Bollweevil. All of them's last name was something that only they themselves and the priest could pronounce. All she could make out of it was Gobblehook. She and Mrs. McIntyre had been calling them the Gobblehooks all week while they got ready for them.

There had been a great deal to do to get ready for them because they didn't have anything of their own, not a stick of furniture or a sheet or a dish, and everything had had to be scraped together out of things that Mrs. McIntyre couldn't use any more herself. They had collected a piece of odd furniture here and a piece there and they had taken some flowered chicken feed sacks and made curtains for the windows, two red and one green, because they had not had enough of the red sacks to go around. Mrs. McIntyre said she was not made of money and she could not afford to buy curtains. "They can't talk," Mrs. Shortley said. "You reckon they'll know what colors even is?" and Mrs. McIntyre had said that after what those people had been through, they should be grateful for anything they could get. She said to think how lucky they were to escape from over there and come to a place like this.

Mrs. Shortley recalled a newsreel she had seen once of a small room piled high with bodies of dead naked people all in a heap, their arms and legs tangled together, a head thrust in here, a head there, a foot, a knee, a part that should have been covered up sticking out, a hand raised clutching nothing. Before you could realize that it was real and take it into your head, the picture changed and a hollow-sounding voice was saying, "Time marches on!" This was the kind of thing that was happening every day in Europe where they had not advanced as in this country, and watching from her vantage point, Mrs. Shortley had the sudden intuition that the Gobblehooks, like rats with typhoid fleas, could have carried all those murderous ways over the water with them directly to this place. If they had come from where that kind of thing was done to them, who was to say they were not the kind that would also do it to others? The width and breadth of this question nearly shook her. Her stomach trembled as if there had been a slight quake in the heart of the mountain and automatically she moved down from her elevation and went forward to be introduced to them, as if she meant to find out at once what they were capable of.

She approached, stomach foremost, head back, arms folded, boots flopping gently against her large legs. About fifteen feet from the gesticulating group, she stopped and made her presence felt by training her gaze on the back of Mrs. McIntyre's neck. Mrs. McIntyre was a small woman of sixty with a round wrinkled face and red bangs that came almost down to two high orange-colored penciled eyebrows. She had a little doll's mouth and eyes that were a soft blue when she opened them wide but more like steel or granite when she narrowed them to inspect a milk can. She had buried one husband and divorced two and Mrs. Shortley respected her as a person nobody had put anything over on yet-except, ha, ha, perhaps the Shortleys. She held out her arm in Mrs. Shortley's direction and said to the Rudolph boy, "And this is Mrs. Shortley. Mr. Shortley is my dairyman. Where's Mr. Shortley?" she asked as his wife began to approach again, her arms still folded. "I want him to meet the Guizacs."

Now it was Guizac. She wasn't calling them Gobblehook to their face. "Chancey's at the barn," Mrs. Shortley said. "He don't have time to rest himself in the bushes like them niggers over there."

Her look first grazed the tops of the displaced people's heads and then revolved downwards slowly, the way a buzzard glides and drops in the air until it alights on the carcass. She stood far enough away so that the man would not be able to kiss her hand. He looked directly at her with little green eyes and gave her a broad grin that was toothless on one side. Mrs. Shortley, without smiling, turned her attention to the little girl who stood by the mother, swinging her shoulders from side to side. She had long braided hair in two looped pigtails and there was no denying she was a pretty child even if she did have a bug's name. She was better looking than either Annie Maude or Sarah Mae, Mrs. Shortley's two girls going on fifteen and seventeen but Annie Maude had never got her growth and Sarah Mae had a cast in her eye. She compared the foreign boy to her son, H.C., and H.C. came out far ahead. H.C. was twenty years old with her build and eyeglasses. He was going to Bible school now and when he finished he was going to start him a church. He had a strong sweet voice for hymns and could sell anything. Mrs. Shortley looked at the priest and was reminded that these people did not have an advanced religion. There was no telling what all they believed since none of the foolishness had been reformed out of it. Again she saw the room piled high with bodies.

The priest spoke in a foreign way himself, English but as if he had a throatful of hay. He had a big nose and a bald rectangular face and head. While she was observing him, his large mouth dropped open and with a stare behind her, he said, "Arrrrrrr!" and pointed.

Mrs. Shortley spun around. The peacock was standing a few feet behind her, with his head slightly cocked.

"What a beauti-ful birdrrrd!" the priest murmured.

"Another mouth to feed," Mrs. McIntyre said, glancing in the peafowl's direction.

"And when does he raise his splendid tail?" asked the priest.

"Just when it suits him," she said. "There used to be twenty or thirty of those things on the place but I've let them die off. I don't like to hear them scream in the middle of the night."

"So beauti-ful," the priest said. "A tail full of suns," and he crept forward on tiptoe and looked down on the bird's back where the polished gold and green design began. The peacock stood still as if he had just come down from some sun-drenched height to be a vision for them all. The priest's homely red face hung over him, glowing with pleasure.

Mrs. Shortley's mouth had drawn acidly to one side. "Nothing but a peachicken," she muttered.

Mrs. McIntyre raised her orange eyebrows and exchanged a look with her to indicate that the old man was in his second childhood. "Well, we must show the Guizacs their new home," she said impatiently and she herded them into the car again. The peacock stepped off toward the mulberry tree where the two Negroes were hiding and the priest turned his absorbed face away and got in the car and drove the displaced people down to the shack they were to occupy.

Mrs. Shortley waited until the car was out of sight and then she made her way circuitously to the mulberry tree and stood about ten feet behind the two Negroes, one an old man holding a bucket half full of calf feed and the other a yellowish boy with a short woodchuck-like head pushed into a rounded felt hat. "Well," she said slowly, "yawl have looked long enough. What you think about them?"

The old man, Astor, raised himself. "We been watching," he said as if this would be news to her. "Who they now?"

"They come from over the water," Mrs. Shortley said with a wave of her arm. "They're what is called Displaced Persons."

"Displaced Persons," he said. "Well now. I declare. What do that mean?"

"It means they ain't-where they were born at and there's nowhere for them to go-like if you was run out of here and wouldn't nobody have you."

"It seem like they here, though," the old man said in a reflective voice. "If they here, they somewhere."

"Sho is," the other agreed. "They here."

The illogic of Negro-thinking always irked Mrs. Shortley. "They ain't where they belong to be at," she said. "They belong to be back over yonder where everything is still like they been used to. Over here it's more advanced than where they come from. But yawl better look out now," she said and nodded her head. "There's about ten million billion more just like them and I know what Mrs. McIntyre said."

"Say what?" the young one asked.

"Places are not easy to get nowadays, for white or black, but I reckon I heard what she stated to me," she said in a sing-song voice.

"You liable to hear most anything," the old man remarked, leaning forward as if he were about to walk off but holding himself suspended.

"I heard her say, 'This is going to put the Fear of the Lord into those shiftless niggers!'" Mrs. Shortley said in a ringing voice.

The old man started off. "She say something like that every now and then," he said. "Ha. Ha. Yes indeed."

"You better get on in that barn and help Mr. Shortley," she said to the other one. "What you reckon she pays you for?"

"He the one sont me out," the Negro muttered. "He the one gimme something else to do."

"Well you better get to doing it then," she said and stood there until he moved off. Then she stood a while longer, reflecting, her unseeing eyes directly in front of the peacock's tail. He had jumped into the tree and his tail hung in front of her, full of fierce planets with eyes that were each ringed in green and set against a sun that was gold in one second's light and salmon-colored in the next. She might have been looking at a map of the universe but she didn't notice it any more than she did the spots of sky that cracked the dull green of the tree. She was having an inner vision instead. She was seeing the ten million billion of them pushing their way into new places over here and herself, a giant angel with wings as wide as a house, telling the Negroes that they would have to find another place. She turned herself in the direction of the barn, musing on this, her expression lofty and satisfied.

She approached the barn from an oblique angle that allowed her a look in the door before she could be seen herself. Mr. Chancey Shortley was adjusting the last milking machine on a large black and white spotted cow near the entrance, squatting at her heels. There was about a half-inch of cigarette adhering to the center of his lower lip. Mrs. Shortley observed it minutely for half a second. "If she seen or heard of you smoking in this barn, she would blow a fuse," she said.

Mr. Shortley raised a sharply rutted face containing a washout under each cheek and two long crevices eaten down both sides of his blistered mouth. "You gonter be the one to tell her?" he asked.

"She's got a nose of her own," Mrs. Shortley said.

Mr. Shortley, without appearing to give the feat any consideration, lifted the cigarette stub with the sharp end of his tongue, drew it into his mouth, closed his lips tightly, rose, stepped out, gave his wife a good round appreciative stare, and spit the smoldering butt into the grass.

"Aw Chancey," she said, "haw haw," and she dug a little hole for it with her toe and covered it up. This trick of Mr. Shortley's was actually his way of making love to her. When he had done his courting, he had not brought a guitar to strum or anything pretty for her to keep, but had sat on her porch steps, not saying a word, imitating a paralyzed man propped up to enjoy a cigarette. When the cigarette got the proper size, he would turn his eyes to her and open his mouth and draw in the butt and then sit there as if he had swallowed it, looking at her with the most loving look anybody could imagine. It nearly drove her wild and every time he did it, she wanted to pull his hat down over his eyes and hug him to death.

"Well," she said, going into the barn after him, "the Gobblehooks have come and she wants you to meet them, says, 'Where's Mr. Shortley?' and I says, 'He don't have time...'"

"Tote up them weights," Mr. Shortley said, squatting to the cow again.

"You reckon he can drive a tractor when he don't know English?" she asked. "I don't think she's going to get her money's worth out of them. That boy can talk but he looks delicate. The one can work can't talk and the one can talk can't work. She ain't any better off than if she had more niggers."

"I rather have a nigger if it was me," Mr. Shortley said.

"She says it's ten million more like them, Displaced Persons, she says that there priest can get her all she wants."

"She better quit messin with that there priest," Mr. Shortley said.

"He don't look smart," Mrs. Shortley said, "–kind of foolish."

"I ain't going to have the Pope of Rome tell me how to run no dairy,"
Mr. Shortley said.

"They ain't Eye-talians, they're Poles," she said. "From Poland where all them bodies were stacked up at. You remember all them bodies?"

"I give them three weeks here," Mr. Shortley said.

Three weeks later Mrs. McIntyre and Mrs. Shortley drove to the cane bottom to see Mr. Guizac start to operate the silage cutter, a new machine that Mrs. McIntyre had just bought because she said, for the first time, she had somebody who could operate it. Mr. Guizac could drive a tractor, use the rotary hay-baler, the silage cutter, the combine, the letz mill, or any other machine she had on the place. He was an expert mechanic, a carpenter, and a mason. He was thrifty and energetic. Mrs. McIntyre said she figured he would save her twenty dollars a month on repair bills alone. She said getting him was the best day's work she had ever done in her life. He could work milking machines and he was scrupulously clean. He did not smoke.

She parked her car on the edge of the cane field and they got out. Sulk, the young Negro, was attaching the wagon to the cutter and Mr. Guizac was attaching the cutter to the tractor. He finished first and pushed the colored boy out of the way and attached the wagon to the cutter himself, gesticulating with a bright angry face when he wanted the hammer or the screwdriver. Nothing was done quick enough to suit him. The Negroes made him nervous.

13

The week before, he had come upon Sulk at the dinner hour, sneaking with a croker sack into the pen where the young turkeys were. He had watched him take a frying-size turkey from the lot and thrust it in the sack and put the sack under his coat. Then he had followed him around the barn, jumped on him, dragged him to Mrs. McIntyre's back door and had acted out the entire scene for her, while the Negro muttered and grumbled and said God might strike him dead if he had been stealing any turkey, he had only been taking it to put some black shoe polish on its head because it had the sorehead. God might strike him dead if that was not the truth before Jesus. Mrs. McIntyre told him to go put the turkey back and then she was a long time explaining to the Pole that all Negroes would steal. She finally had to call Rudolph and tell him in English and have him tell his father in Polish, and Mr. Guizac had gone off with a startled disappointed face.

Mrs. Shortley stood by hoping there would be trouble with the silage machine but there was none. All of Mr. Guizac's motions were quick and accurate. He jumped on the tractor like a monkey and maneuvered the big orange cutter into the cane; in a second the silage was spurting in a green let out of the pipe into the wagon. He went jolting down the row until his disappeared from sight and the noise became remote.

Mrs. McIntyre sighed with pleasure. "At last," she said, "I've got somebody I can depend on. For years I've been fooling with sorry people. Sorry people. Poor white trash and niggers," she muttered. "They've drained me dry. Before you all came I had Ringfields and Collins and Jarrells and Perkins and Pinkins and Herrins and God knows what all else and not a one of them left without taking something off this place that didn't belong to them. Not a one!"

Mrs. Shortley could listen to this with composure because she knew that if Mrs. McIntyre had considered her trash, they couldn't have talked about trashy people together. Neither of them approved of trash. Mrs. McIntyre continued with the monologue that Mrs. Shortley had heard oftentimes before. "I've been running this place for thirty years," she said, looking with a deep frown out over the field, "and always just barely making it. People think you're made of money. I have taxes to pay. I have the insurance to keep up. I have the repair bills. I have the feed bills." It all gathered up and she stood with her chest lifted and her small hands gripped around her elbows. "Ever since the judge died," she said, "I've barely been making ends meet and they all take something when they leave. The niggers don't leave—they stay and steal. A nigger thinks anybody is rich he can steal from and that white trash thinks anybody is rich who can afford to hire people as sorry as they are. And all I've got is the dirt under my feet!"

You hire and fire, Mrs. Shortley thought, but she didn't always say what she thought. She stood by and let Mrs. McIntyre say it all out to the end but this time it didn't end as usual. "But at last I'm saved!" Mrs. McIntyre said. "One fellow's misery is the other fellow's gain. That man there," and she pointed where the Displaced Person had disappeared, "—he has to work! He wants to work!" She turned to Mrs. Shortley with her bright wrinkled face. "That man is my salvation!" she said.

Mrs. Shortley looked straight ahead as if her vision penetrated the cane and the hill and pierced through to the other side. "I would suspicion salvation got from the devil," she said in a slow detached way.

"Now what do you mean by that?" Mrs. McIntyre asked, looking at her sharply.

14

Mrs. Shortley wagged her head but would not say anything else. The fact was she had nothing else to say for this intuition had only at that instant come to her. She had never given much thought to the devil for she felt that religion was essentially for those people who didn't have the brains to avoid evil without it. For people like herself, for people of gumption, it was a social occasion providing the opportunity to sing; but if she had ever given it much thought, she would have considered the devil the head of it and God the hanger-on. With the coming of these displaced people, she was obliged to give new thought to a good many things.

"I know what Sledgewig told Annie Maude," she said, and when Mrs. McIntyre carefully did not ask her what but reached down and broke off a sprig of sassafras to chew; she continued in a way to indicate she was not telling all, "that they wouldn't be able to live long, the four of them, on seventy dollars a month."

"He's worth raising," Mrs. McIntyre said. "He saves me money."

This was as much as to say that Chancey had never saved her money. Chancey got up at four in the morning to milk her cows, in winter wind and summer heat, and he had been doing it for the last two years. They had been with her the longest she had ever had anybody. The gratitude they got was these hints that she hadn't been saved any money.

"Is Mr. Shortley feeling better today?" Mrs. McIntyre asked.

Mrs. Shortley thought it was about time she was asking that question. Mr. Shortley had been in bed two days with an attack. Mr. Guizac had taken his place in the dairy in addition to doing his own work. "No he ain't," she said. "That doctor said he was suffering from over-exhaustion."

"If Mr. Shortley is over-exhausted," Mrs. McIntyre said, "then he must have a second job on the side," and she looked at Mrs. Shortley with almost closed eyes as if she were examining the bottom of a milk can.

Mrs. Shortley did not say a word but her dark suspicion grew like a black thunder cloud. The fact was that Mr. Shortley did have a second job on the side and that, in a free country, this was none of Mrs. McIntyre's business. Mr. Shortley made whisky. He had a small still back in the farthest reaches of the place, on Mrs. McIntyre's land to be sure, but on land that she only owned and did not cultivate, on idle land that was not doing anybody any good. Mr. Shortley was not afraid of work. He got up at four in the morning and milked her cows and in the middle of the day when he was supposed to be resting, he was off attending to his still. Not every man would work like that. The Negroes knew about his still but he knew about theirs so there had never been any disagreeableness between them. But with foreigners on the place, with people who were all eyes and no understanding, who had come from a place continually fighting, where the religion had not been reformed-with this kind of people, you had to be on the lookout every minute. She thought there ought to be a law against them. There was no reason they couldn't stay over there and take the places of some of the people who had been killed in their wars and butcherings.

"What's furthermore," she said suddenly, "Sledgewig said as soon as her papa saved the money, he was going to buy him a used car. Once they get them a used car, they'll leave you."

"I can't pay him enough for him to save money," Mrs. McIntyre said. "I'm not worrying about that. Of course," she said then, "if Mr. Shortley got incapacitated, I would have to use Mr. Guizac in the dairy all the time and I would have to pay him more. He doesn't smoke," she said, and it was the fifth time within the week that she had pointed this out.

15

"It is no man," Mrs. Shortley said emphatically, "that works as hard as Chancey, or is as easy with a cow, or is more of a Christian," and she folded her arms and her gaze pierced the distance. The noise of the tractor and cutter increased and Mr. Guizac appeared coming around the other side of the cane row. "Which can not be said about everybody," she muttered. She wondered whether, if the Pole found Chancey's still, he would know what it was. The trouble with these people was, you couldn't tell what they knew. Every time Mr. Guizac smiled, Europe stretched out in Mrs. Shortley's imagination, mysterious and evil, the devil's experiment station.

The tractor, the cutter, the wagon passed, rattling and rumbling and grinding before them. "Think how long that would have taken with men and mules to do it," Mrs. McIntyre shouted. "We'll get this whole bottom cut within two days at this rate."

"Maybe," Mrs. Shortley muttered, "if don't no terrible accident occur." She thought how the tractor had made mules worthless. Nowadays you couldn't give away a mule. The next thing to go, she reminded herself, will be niggers.

In the afternoon she explained what was going to happen to them to Astor and Sulk who were in the cow lot, filling the manure spreader. She sat down next to the block of salt under a small shed, her stomach in her lap, her arms on top of it. "All you colored people better look out," she said. "You know how much you can get for a mule."

"Nothing, no indeed," the old man said, "not one thing."

"Before it was a tractor," she said, "it could be a mule. And before it was a Displaced Person, it could be a nigger. The time is going to come," she prophesied, "when it won't be no more occasion to speak of a nigger."

The old man laughed politely. "Yes indeed," he said. "Ha ha."

The young one didn't say anything. He only looked sullen but when she had gone in the house, he said, "Big Belly act like she know everything."

"Never mind," the old man said, "your place too low for anybody to dispute with you for it."

She didn't tell her fears about the still to Mr. Shortley until he was back on the job in the dairy. Then one night after they were in bed, she said, "That man prowls."

Mr. Shortley folded his hands on his bony chest and pretended he was a corpse.

"Prowls," she continued and gave him a sharp kick in the side with her knee. "Who's to say what they know and don't know? Who's to say if he found it he wouldn't go right to her and tell? How you know they don't make liquor in Europe? They drive tractors. They got them all kinds of machinery. Answer me."

"Don't worry me now," Mr. Shortley said. "I'm a dead man."

"It's them little eyes of his that's foreign," she muttered. "And that way he's got of shrugging." She drew her shoulders up and shrugged several times. "How come he's got anything to shrug about?" she asked.

"If everybody was as dead as I am, nobody would have no trouble," Mr. Shortley said.

"That priest," she muttered and was silent for a minute. Then she said, "In Europe they probably got some different way to make liquor but I reckon they know all the ways. They're full of crooked ways. They never have advanced or reformed. They got the same religion as a thousand years ago. It could only be the devil responsible for that. Always fighting amongst each other. Disputing. And then get us into it. Ain't they got us into it twict already and we ain't got no more sense than to go over there and settle it for them and then they come on back over here and snoop around and find your still and go straight to her. And liable to kiss her hand any minute. Do you hear me?"

"No," Mr. Shortley said.

"And I'll tell you another thing," she said. "I wouldn't be a tall surprised if he don't know everything you say, whether it be in English or not."

"I don't speak no other language," Mr. Shortley murmured.

"I suspect," she said, "that before long there won't be no more niggers on this place. And I tell you what. I'd rather have niggers than them Poles. And what's furthermore, I aim to take up for the niggers when the time comes. When Gobblehook first come here, you recollect how he shook their hands, like he didn't know the difference, like he might have been as black as them, but when it come to finding out Sulk was taking turkeys, he gone on and told her. I known he was taking turkeys. I could have told her myself."

Mr. Shortley was breathing softly as if he were asleep.

"A nigger don't know when he has a friend," she said. "And I'll tell you another thing. I get a heap out of Sledgewig. Sledgewig said that in Poland they lived in a brick house and one night a man come and told them to get out of it before daylight. Do you believe they ever lived in a brick house?

"Airs," she said. "That's just airs. A wooden house is good enough for me. Chancey," she said, "turn thisaway. I hate to see niggers mistreated and run out. I have a heap of pity for niggers and poor folks. Ain't I always had?" she asked. "I say ain't I always been a friend to niggers and poor folks?

"When the time comes," she said, "I'll stand up for the niggers and that's that. I ain't going to see that priest drive out all the niggers."

Mrs. McIntyre bought a new drag harrow and a tractor with a power lift because she said, for the first time, she had someone who could handle machinery. She and Mrs. Shortley had driven to the back field to inspect what he had harrowed the day before. "That's been done beautifully!" Mrs. McIntyre said, looking out over the red undulating ground.

Mrs. McIntyre had changed since the Displaced Person had been working for her and Mrs. Shortley had observed the change very closely: she had begun to act like somebody who was getting rich secretly and she didn't confide in Mrs. Shortley the way she used to. Mrs. Shortley suspected that the priest was at the bottom of the change. They were very slick. First he would get her into his Church and then he would get his hand in her pocketbook. Well, Mrs. Shortley thought, the more fool she! Mrs. Shortley had a secret herself. She knew something the Displaced Person was doing that would floor Mrs. McIntyre. "I still say he ain't going to work forever for seventy dollars a month," she murmured. She intended to keep her secret to herself and Mr. Shortley.

"Well," Mrs. McIntyre said, "I may have to get rid of some of this other help so I can pay him more."

Mrs. Shortley nodded to indicate she had known this for some time. "I'm not saying those niggers ain't had it coming," she said. "But they do the best they know how. You can always tell a nigger what to do and stand by until he does it."

"That's what the judge said," Mrs. McIntyre said and looked at her with approval. The Judge was her first husband, the one who had left her the place. Mrs. Shortley had heard that she had married him when she was thirty and he

17

was seventy-five, thinking she would be rich as soon as he died, but the old man was a scoundrel and when his estate was settled, they found he didn't have a nickel. All he left her were the fifty acres and the house. But she always spoke of him in a reverent way and quoted his sayings, such as, "One fellow's misery is the other fellow's gain," and "The devil you know is better than the devil you don't."

"However," Mrs. Shortley remarked, "the devil you know is better than the devil you don't," and she had to turn away so that Mrs. McIntyre would not see her smile. She had found out what the Displaced Person was up to through the old man, Astor, and she had not told anybody but Mr. Shortley. Mr. Shortley had risen straight up in bed like Lazarus from the tomb.

"Shut your mouth!" he had said.

"Yes," she had said.

"Naw!" Mr. Shortley had said.

"Yes," she had said.

Mr. Shortley had fallen back flat.

"The Pole don't know any better," Mrs. Shortley had said. "I reckon that priest is putting him up to it is all. I blame the priest."

The priest came frequently to see the Guizacs and he would always stop in and visit Mrs. McIntyre too and they would walk around the place and she would point out her improvements and listen to his rattling talk. It suddenly came to Mrs. Shortley that he was trying to persuade her to bring another Polish family onto the place. With two of them here, there would be almost nothing spoken but Polish! The Negroes would be gone and there would be the two families against Mr. Shortley and herself! She began to imagine a war of words, to see the Polish words and the English words coming at each other, stalking forward, not sentences, just words, gabble gabble gabble, flung out high and shrill and stalking forward and then grappling with each other. She saw the Polish words, dirty and all- knowing and unreformed, flinging mud on the clean English words until everything was equally dirty. She saw them all piled up in a room, all the dead dirty words, theirs and hers too, piled up like the naked bodies in the newsreel. God save me, she cried silently, from the stinking power of Satan! And she started from that day to read her Bible with a new attention. She poured over the Apocalypse and began to quote from the Prophets and before long she had come to a deeper understanding of her existence. She saw plainly that the meaning of the world was a mystery that had been planned and she was not surprised to suspect that she had a special part in the plan because she was strong. She saw that the Lord God Almighty had created the strong people to do what had to be done and she felt that she would be ready when she was called. Right now she felt that her business was to watch the priest.

His visits irked her more and more. On the last one, he went about picking up feathers off the ground. He found two peacock feathers and four or five turkey feathers and an old brown hen feather and took them off with him like a bouquet. This foolish-acting did not deceive Mrs. Shortley any. Here he was: leading foreigners over in hordes to places that were not theirs, to cause disputes, to uproot niggers, to plant the Whore of Babylon in the midst of the righteous! Whenever he came on the place, she hid herself behind something and watched until he left.

It was on a Sunday afternoon that she had her vision. She had gone to drive in the cows for Mr. Shortley who had a pain in his knee and she was walking slowly through the pasture, her arms folded, her eyes on the distant low-lying clouds that looked like rows and rows of white fish washed up on a great blue beach. She paused after an incline to heave a sigh of exhaustion for she had an immense weight to carry around and she was not as young as she used to be. At times she could feel her heart, like a child's fist, clenching and unclenching inside her chest, and when the feeling came, it stopped her thought altogether and she would go about like a large hull of herself, moving for no reason; but she gained this incline without a tremor and stood at the top of it, pleased with herself. Suddenly while she watched, the sky folded back in two pieces like the curtain to a stage and a gigantic figure stood facing her. It was the color of the sun in the early afternoon, white-gold. It was of no definite shape but there were fiery wheels with fierce dark eyes in them, spinning rapidly all around it. She was not able to tell if the figure was going forward or backward because its magnificence was so great. She shut her eyes in order to look at it and it turned blood-red and the wheels turned white. A voice, very resonant, said the one word, "Prophesy!"

She stood there, tottering slightly but still upright, her eyes shut tight and her fists clenched and her straw sun hat low on her forehead. "The children of wicked nations will be butchered," she said in a loud voice. "Legs where arms should be, foot to face, ear in the palm of hand. Who will remain whole? Who will remain whole? Who?"

Presently she opened her eyes. The sky was full of white fish carried lazily on their sides by some invisible current and pieces of the sun, submerged some distance beyond them, appeared from time to time as if they were being washed in the opposite direction. Woodenly she planted one foot in front of the other until she had crossed the pasture and reached the lot. She walked through the barn like one in a daze and did not speak to Mr. Shortley. She continued up the road until she saw the priest's car parked in front of Mrs. McIntyre's house. "Here again," she muttered. "Come to destroy."

Mrs. McIntyre and the priest were walking in the yard. In order not to meet them face to face, she turned to the left and entered the feed house, a single-room shack piled on one side with flowered sacks of scratch feed. There were spilled oyster shells in one corner and a few old dirty calendars on the wall, advertising calf feed and various patent medicine remedies. One showed a bearded gentleman in a frock coat, holding up a bottle, and beneath his feet was the inscription, "I have been made regular by this marvelous discovery." Mrs. Shortley had always felt close to this man as if he were some distinguished person she was acquainted with but now her mind was on nothing but the dangerous presence of the priest. She stationed herself at a crack between two boards where she could look out and see him and Mrs. McIntyre strolling toward the turkey brooder, which was placed just outside the feed house.

"Arrrrr!" he said as they approached the brooder. "Look at the little biddies!" and he stooped and squinted through the wire.

Mrs. Shortley's mouth twisted.

"Do you think the Guizacs will want to leave me?" Mrs. McIntyre asked. "Do you think they'll go to Chicago or some place like that?"

"And why should they do that now?" asked the priest, wiggling his finger at a turkey, his big nose close to the wire.

"Money," Mrs. McIntyre said.

"Arrrr, give them some morrre then," he said indifferently. "They have to get along."

"So do I," Mrs. McIntyre muttered. "It means I'm going to have to get rid of some of these others."

19

"And arrre the Shortleys satisfactory?" he inquired, paying more attention to the turkeys than to her.

"Five times in the last month I've found Mr. Shortley smoking in the barn," Mrs. McIntyre said. "Five times."

"And arrre the Negroes any better?"

"They lie and steal and have to be watched all the time," she said.

"Tsk, tsk," he said. "Which will you discharge?"

"I've decided to give Mr. Shortley his month's notice tomorrow," Mrs. McIntyre said.

The priest scarcely seemed to hear her he was so busy wiggling his finger inside the wire. Mrs. Shortley sat down on an open sack of laying mash with a dead thump that sent feed dust clouding up around her. She found herself looking straight ahead at the opposite wall where the gentleman on the calendar was holding up his marvelous discovery but she didn't see him. She looked ahead as if she saw nothing whatsoever. Then she rose and ran to her house. Her face was an almost volcanic red.

She opened all the drawers and dragged out boxes and old battered suitcases from under the bed. She began to unload the drawers into the boxes, all the time without pause, without taking off the sunhat she had on her head. She set the two girls to doing the same. When Mr. Shortley came in, she did not even look at him but merely pointed one arm at him while she packed with the other. "Bring the car around to the back door," she said. "You ain't waiting to be fired!"

Mr. Shortley had never in his life doubted her omniscience. He perceived the entire situation in half a second and, with only a sour scowl, retreated out the door and went to drive the automobile around to the back.

They tied the two iron beds to the top of the car and the two rocking chairs inside the beds and rolled the two mattresses up between the rocking chairs. On top of this they tied a crate of chickens. They loaded the inside of the car with the old suitcases and boxes, leaving a small space for Annie Maude and Sarah Mae. It took them the rest of the afternoon and half the night to do this but Mrs. Shortley was determined that they would leave before four o'clock in the morning, that Mr. Shortley should not adjust another milking machine on this place. All the time she had been working, her face was changing rapidly from red to white and back again.

Just before dawn, as it began to drizzle rain, they were ready to leave. They all got in the car and sat there cramped up between boxes and bundles and rolls of bedding. The square black automobile moved off with more than its customary grinding noises as if it were protesting the load. In the back, the two long bony yellow-haired girls were sitting on a pile of boxes and there was a beagle hound puppy and a cat with two kittens somewhere under the blankets. The car moved slowly, like some overfreighted leaking ark, away from their shack and past the white house where Mrs. McIntyre was sleeping soundly-hardly guessing that her cows would not be milked by Mr. Shortley that morning-and past the Pole's shack on top of the hill and on down the road to the gate where the two Negroes were walking, one behind the other, on their way to help with the milking. They looked straight at the car and its occupants but even as the dim yellow headlights lit up their faces, they politely did not seem to see anything, or anyhow, to attach significance to what was there. The loaded car might have been passing mist in the early morning half-light. They continued up the road at the same even pace without looking back.

A dark yellow sun was beginning to rise in a sky that was the same slick dark gray as the highway. The fields stretched away, stiff and weedy, on either side.

"Where we goin?" Mr. Shortley asked for the first time.

Mrs. Shortley sat with one foot on a packing box so that her knee was pushed into her stomach. Mr. Shortley's elbow was almost under her nose and Sarah Mae's bare left foot was sticking over the front seat, touching her ear.

"Where we goin?" Mr. Shortley repeated and when she didn't answer again, he turned and looked at her.

Fierce heat seemed to be swelling slowly and fully into her face as if it were welling up now for a final assault. She was sitting in an erect way in spite of the fact that one leg was twisted under her and one knee was almost into her neck, but there was a peculiar lack of light in her icy blue eyes. All the vision in them might have been turned around, looking inside her. She suddenly grabbed Mr. Shortley's elbow and Sarah Mae's foot at the same time and began to tug and pull on them as if she were trying to fit the two extra limbs onto herself.

Mr. Shortley began to curse and quickly stopped the car and Sarah Mae yelled to quit but Mrs. Shortley apparently intended to rearrange the whole car at once. She thrashed forward and backward, clutching at everything she could get her hands on and hugging it to herself, Mr. Shortley's head, Sarah Mae's leg, the cat, a wad of white bedding, her own big moon-like knee; then all at once her fierce expression faded into a look of astonishment and her grip on what she had loosened. One of her eyes drew near to the other and seemed to collapse quietly and she was still.

The two girls, who didn't know what had happened to her, began to say, "Where we goin, Ma? Where we goin?" They thought she was playing a joke and that their father, staring straight ahead at her, was imitating a dead man. They didn't know that she had had a great experience or ever been displaced in the world from all that belonged to her. They were frightened by the gray slick road before them and they kept repeating in higher and higher voices, "Where we goin, Ma? Where we goin?" while their mother, her huge body rolled back still against the seat and her eyes like blue-painted glass, seemed to contemplate for the first time the tremendous frontiers of her true country.

Answer *true* or *false* for each of the following statements.

1.42 _____ The Shortleys, the Negroes, and the Guizacs are Mrs. McIntyre's hired help.

1.43 _____ The mayor brought the Displaced Person and his family to Mrs. McIntyre's farm.

1.44 _____ The Guizacs are from a foreign country.

1.45 _____ Mrs. McIntyre wants all the peacocks to die off.

1.46 _____ Mr. Guizac wanted to work.

1.47 _____ Mrs. Shortley, seeing Mr. Guizac's desire to work hard, declared, "That man is my salvation!"

1.48 _____ Mrs. Shortley believed that Mr. Guizac was from the devil.

1.49 _____ Mrs. Guizac believed that religion was for people who were not smart enough to avoid evil without it.

1.50 _____ Mrs. Guizac believed that displaced persons would soon replace black people.

1.51 _____ Mrs. Shortley thinks of herself and her husband as Christian people who are friends to "niggers and poor folks."

1.52 _____ Mr. Guizac spends most of his time spying on the Shortleys and complaining to Mrs. McIntyre.

1.53   _____ Mrs. McIntyre married the Judge thinking that she would be rich as soon as he died.

1.54   _____ Mrs. Shortley prophesies, "The children of the wicked will be butchered!"

1.55   _____ The priest came to visit the Guizacs regularly.

1.56   _____ The Guizacs leave Mrs. McIntyre's farm before they are fired.

1.57   _____ Unsure of their destination, Mr. Shortley and his daughters repeatedly ask Mrs. Shortley, "Where are we going?"

Section 2 — Displaced Person

"Well," Mrs. McIntyre said to the old Negro, "we can get along without them. We've seen them come and seen them go-black and white." She was standing in the calf barn while he cleaned it and she held a rake in her hand and now and then pulled a corn cob from a corner or pointed to a soggy spot that he had missed. When she discovered the Shortleys were gone, she was delighted as it meant she wouldn't have to fire them. The people she hired always left her-because they were that kind of people. Of all the families she had had, the Shortleys were the best if she didn't count the Displaced Person. They had been not quite trash; Mrs. Shortley was a good woman, and she would miss her but as the Judge used to say, you couldn't have your pie and eat it too, and she was satisfied with the D.P. "We've seen them come and seen them go," she repeated with satisfaction.

"And me and you," the old man said, stooping to drag his hoe under a feed rack, "is still here."

She caught exactly what he meant her to catch in his tone. Bars of sunlight fell from the cracked ceiling across his back and cut him in three distinct parts. She watched his long hands clenched around the hoe and his crooked old profile pushed close to them. You might have been here before I was, she said to herself, but it's mighty likely I'll be here when you're gone. "I've spent half my life fooling with worthless people," she said in a severe voice, "but now I'm through."

"Black and white," he said, "is the same."

"I am through," she repeated and gave her dark smock that she had thrown over her shoulders like a cape a quick snatch at the neck. She had on a broad-brimmed black straw hat that had cost her twenty dollars twenty years ago and that she used now for a sunhat. "Money is the root of all evil," she said. "The Judge said so every day. He said he deplored money. He said the reason you niggers were so uppity was because there was so much money in circulation."

The old Negro had known the judge. "Judge say he long for the day when he be too poor to pay a nigger to work," he said. "Say when that day come, the world be back on its feet."

She leaned forward, her hands on her hips and her neck stretched and said, "Well that day has almost come around here and I'm telling each and every one of you: you better look sharp. I don't have to put up with foolishness any more. I have somebody now who *has* to work!"

The old man knew when to answer and when not. At length he said, "We seen them come and we seen them go."

"However, the Shortleys were not the worst by far," she said. "I well remember those Garrits."

"They was before them Collinses," he said.

"No, before the Ringfields."

"Sweet Lord, them Ringfields!" he murmured.

"None of that kind *want* to work," she said.

"We seen them come and we seen them go," he said as if this were a refrain. "But we ain't never had one before," he said, bending himself up until he faced her, "like what we got now." He was cinnamon-colored with eyes that were so blurred with age that they seemed to be hung behind cobwebs.

She gave him an intense stare and held it until, lowering his hands on the hoe, he bent down again and dragged a pile of shavings alongside the wheelbarrow. She said stiffly, "He can wash out that barn in the time it took Mr. Shortley to make up his mind he had to do it."

"He from Pole," the old man muttered.

"From Poland."

"In Pole it ain't like it is here," he said. "They got different ways of doing," and he began to mumble unintelligibly.

"What are you saying?" she said. "If you have anything to say about him, say it and say it aloud."

He was silent, bending his knees precariously and edging the rake along the underside of the trough.

"If you know anything he's done that he shouldn't, I expect you to report it to me," she said.

"It warn't like it was what he should ought or oughtn't," he muttered. "It was like what nobody else don't do."

"You don't have anything against him," she said shortly, "and he's here to stay."

"We ain't never had one like him before is all," he murmured and gave his polite laugh.

"Times are changing," she said. "Do you know what's happening to this world? It's swelling up. It's getting so full of people that only the smart thrifty energetic ones are going to survive," and she tapped the words, smart, thrifty, and energetic out on the palm of her hand. Through the far end of the stall she could see down the road to where the Displaced Person was standing in the open barn door with the green hose in his hand. There was a certain stiffness about his figure that seemed to make it necessary for her to approach him slowly, even in her thoughts. She had decided this was because she couldn't hold an easy conversation with him. Whenever she said anything to him, she found herself shouting and nodding extravagantly and she would be conscious that one of the Negroes was leaning behind the nearest shed, watching.

"No indeed!" she said, sitting down on one of the feed racks and folding her arms, "I've made up my mind that I've had enough trashy people on this place to last me a lifetime and I'm not going to spend my last years fooling with Shortleys and Ringfields and Collins when the world is full of people who *have* to work."

"How come they so many extra?" he asked.

"People are selfish," she said. "They have too many children. There's no sense in it any more."

He had picked up the wheelbarrow handles and was backing out the door and he paused, half in the sunlight and half out, and stood there chewing his gums as if he had forgotten which direction he wanted to move in.

"What you colored people don't realize," she said, "is that I'm the one around here who holds all the strings together. If you don't work, I don't make any money and I can't pay you. You're all dependent on me but you each and every one act like the shoe is on the other foot."

It was not possible to tell from his face if he heard her. Finally he backed out with the wheelbarrow. "Judge say the devil he know is better than the devil he don't," he said in a clear mutter and trundled off.

She got up and followed him, a deep vertical pit appearing suddenly in the center of her forehead, just under the red bangs. "The Judge has long since ceased to pay the bills around here," she called in a piercing voice.

He was the only one of her Negroes who had known the judge and he thought this gave him title. He had had a low opinion of Mr. Crooms and Mr. McIntyre, her other husbands, and in his veiled polite way, he had congratulated her after each of her divorces. When he thought it necessary, he would work under a window where he knew she was sitting and talk to himself, a careful roundabout discussion, question and answer and then refrain. Once she had got up silently and slammed the window down so hard that he had fallen backwards off his feet. Or occasionally he spoke with the peacock. The cock would follow him around the place, his steady eye on the ear of corn that stuck up from the old man's back pocket or he would sit near him and pick himself. Once from the open kitchen door, she had heard him say to the bird, "I remember when it was twenty of you walking about this place and now it's only you and two hens. Crooms it was twelve. McIntyre it was five. You and two hens now."

And that time she had stepped out of the door onto the porch and said, "MISTER Crooms and MISTER McIntyre! And I don't want to hear you call either of them anything else again. And you can understand this: when that peachicken dies there won't be any replacements."

She kept the peacock only out of a superstitious fear of annoying the Judge in his grave. He had liked to see them walking around the place for he said they made him feel rich. Of her three husbands, the Judge was the one most present to her although he was the only one she had buried. He was in the family graveyard, a little space fenced in the middle of the back cornfield, with his mother and father and grandfather and three great aunts and two infant cousins. Mr. Crooms, her second, was forty miles away in the state asylum and Mr. McIntyre, her last, was intoxicated, she supposed, in some hotel room in Florida. But the judge, sunk in the cornfield with his family, was always at home.

She had married him when he was an old man and because of his money but there had been another reason that she would not admit then, even to herself: she had liked him. He was a dirty snuff-dipping Court House figure, famous all over the county for being rich, who wore hightop shoes, a string tie, a gray suit with a black stripe in it, and a yellowed panama hat, winter and summer. His teeth and hair were tobacco-colored and his face a clay pink pitted and tracked with mysterious prehistoric-looking marks as if he had been unearthed among fossils. There had been a peculiar odor about him of sweaty fondled bills but he never carried money on him or had a nickel to show. She was his secretary for a few months and the old man with his sharp eye had seen at once that here was a woman who admired him for himself. The three years that he lived after they married were the happiest and most prosperous of Mrs. McIntyre's life, but when he died his estate proved to be bankrupt. He left her a mortgaged house and fifty acres that he had managed to cut the timber off before he died. It was as if, as the final triumph of a successful life, he had been able to take everything with him.

But she had survived. She had survived a succession of tenant farmers and dairymen that the old man himself would have found hard to outdo, and she had been able to meet the constant drain of a tribe of moody unpredictable Negroes, and she had even managed to hold her own against the incidental bloodsuckers, the cattle dealers and lumber men and the buyers and sellers of anything who drove up in pieced-together trucks and honked in the yard.

She stood slightly reared back with her arms folded under her smock and a satisfied expression on her face as she watched the Displaced Person turn off the hose and disappear inside the barn. She was sorry that the poor man had been chased out of Poland and run across Europe and had had to take up in a tenant shack in a strange country, but she had not been responsible for any of this. She had had a hard time herself. She knew what it was to struggle. People ought to have to struggle. Mr. Guizac had probably had everything given to him all the way across Europe and over here. He had probably not had to struggle enough. She had given him a job. She didn't know if he was grateful or not. She didn't know anything about him except that he did the work. The truth was that he was not very real to her yet. He was a kind of miracle that she had seen happen and that she talked about but that she still didn't believe.

She watched as he came out of the barn and motioned to Sulk, who was coming around the back of the lot. He gesticulated and then took something out of his pocket and the two of them stood looking at it. She started down the lane toward them. The Negro's figure was slack and tall and he was craning his round head forward in his usual idiotic way. He was a little better than half-witted but when they were like that they were always good workers. The Judge had said always hire you a half-witted nigger because they don't have sense enough to stop working. The Pole was gesticulating rapidly. He left something with the colored boy and then walked off and before she rounded the turn in the lane, she heard the tractor crank up. He was on his way to the field. The Negro was still hanging there, gaping at whatever he had in his hand.

She entered the lot and walked through the barn, looking with approval at the wet spotless concrete floor. It was only nine-thirty and Mr. Shortley had never got anything washed until eleven. As she came out at the other end, she saw the Negro moving very slowly in a diagonal path across the road in front of her, his eyes still on what Mr. Guizac had given him. He didn't see her and he paused and dipped his knees and leaned over his hand, his tongue describing little circles. He had a photograph. He lifted one finger and traced it lightly over the surface of the picture. Then he looked up and saw her and seemed to freeze, his mouth in a half-grin, his finger lifted.

"Why haven't you gone to the field?" she asked.

He raised one foot and opened his mouth wider while the hand with the photograph edged toward his back pocket.

"What's that?" she said.

"It ain't nothing," he muttered and handed it to her automatically. It was a photograph of a girl of about twelve in a white dress. She had blond hair with a wreath in it and she looked forward out of light eyes that were bland and composed. "Who is this child?" Mrs. McIntyre asked.

"She his cousin," the boy said in a high voice.

"Well what are you doing with it?" she asked.

"She going to mah me," he said in an even higher voice.

"Marry you!" she shrieked.

"I pays half to get her over here," he said. "I pays him three dollar a week. She bigger now. She his cousin. She don't care who she mah she so glad to get away from there." The high voice seemed to shoot up like a nervous let of sound and then fall flat as he watched her face. Her eyes were the color of blue granite when the glare falls on it, but she was not looking at him. She was looking down the road where the distant sound of the tractor could be heard.

"I don't reckon she goin to come nohow," the boy murmured.

"I'll see that you get every cent of your money back," she said in a toneless voice and turned and walked off, holding the photograph bent in two. There was nothing about her small stiff figure to indicate that she was shaken.

As soon as she got in the house, she lay down on her bed and shut her eyes and pressed her hand over her heart as if she were trying to keep it in place. Her mouth opened and she made two or three dry little sounds. Then after a minute she sat up and said aloud, "They're all the same. It's always been like this," and she fell back flat again. "Twenty years of being beaten and done in and they even robbed his grave!" and remembering that, she began to cry quietly, wiping her eyes every now and then with the hem of her smock.

What she had thought of was the angel over the Judge's grave. This had been a naked granite cherub that the old man had seen in the city one day in a tombstone store window. He had been taken with it at once, partly because its face reminded him of his wife and partly because he wanted a genuine work of art over his grave. He had come home with it sitting on the green plush train seat beside him. Mrs. McIntyre had never noticed the resemblance to herself. She had always thought it hideous but when the Herrins stole it off the old man's grave, she was shocked and outraged. Mrs. Herrin had thought it very pretty and had walked to the graveyard frequently to see it, and when the Herrins left the angel left with them, all but its toes, for the ax old man Herrin had used to break it off with had struck slightly too high. Mrs. McIntyre had never been able to afford to have it replaced.

When she had cried all she could, she got up and went into the back hall, a closet-like space that was dark and quiet as a chapel and sat down on the edge of the judge's black mechanical chair with her elbow on his desk. This was a giant roll-top piece of furniture pocked with pigeon holes full of dusty papers. Old bank-books and ledgers were stacked in the half-open drawers and there was a small safe, empty but locked, set like a tabernacle in the center of it. She had left this part of the house unchanged since the old man's time. It was a kind of memorial to him, sacred because he had conducted his business here. With the slightest tilt one way or the other, the chair gave a rusty skeletal groan that sounded something like him when he had complained of his poverty. It had been his first principle to talk as if he were the poorest man in the world and she followed it, not only because he had but because it was true. When she sat with her intense constricted face turned toward the empty safe, she knew there was nobody poorer in the world than she was.

She sat motionless at the desk for ten or fifteen minutes and then as if she had gained some strength, she got up and got in her car and drove to the cornfield.

The road ran through a shadowy pine thicket and ended on top of a hill that rolled fan-wise down and up again in a broad expanse of tassled green. Mr. Guizac was cutting from the outside of the field in a circular path to the center where the graveyard was all but hidden by the corn, and she could see him on the high far side of the slope, mounted on the tractor with the cutter and wagon behind him. From time to time, he had to get off the tractor and climb in the wagon to spread the silage because the Negro had not arrived. She watched impatiently, standing in front of her black coupe with her arms folded under her smock, while he progressed slowly around the rim of the field, gradually getting close enough for her to wave to him to get down. He stopped the machine and jumped off and came running forward, wiping his red jaw with a piece of grease rag.

"I want to talk to you," she said and beckoned him to the edge of the thicket where it was shady. He took off the cap and followed her, smiling, but his smile faded when she turned and faced him. Her eyebrows, thin and fierce as a spider's leg, had drawn together ominously and the deep vertical pit had plunged down from under the red bangs into the bridge of her nose. She removed the bent picture from her pocket and handed it to him silently. Then she stepped back and said, "Mr. Guizac! You would bring this poor innocent child over here and try to marry her to a half-witted thieving black stinking nigger! What kind of a monster are you!"

He took the photograph with a slowly returning smile. "My cousin," he said. "She twelve here. First Communion. Six-ten now."

Monster! she said to herself and looked at him as if she were seeing him for the first time. His forehead and skull were white where they had been protected by his cap but the rest of his face was red and bristled with short yellow hairs. His eyes were like two bright nails behind his gold-rimmed spectacles that had been mended over the nose with haywire. His whole face looked as if it might have been patched together out of several others. "Mr. Guizac," she said, beginning slowly and then speaking faster until she ended breathless in the middle of a word, "that nigger cannot have a white wife from Europe. You can't talk to a nigger that way. You'll excite him and besides it can't be done. Maybe it can be done in Poland but it can't be done here and you'll have to stop. It's all foolishness. That nigger don't have a grain of sense and you'll excite..."

"She in camp three year," he said.

"Your cousin," she said in a positive voice, "cannot come over here and marry one of my Negroes."

"She six-ten year," he said. "From Poland. Mamma die, pappa die. She wait in camp. Three camp." He pulled a wallet from his pocket and fingered through it and took out another picture of the same girl, a few years older, dressed in something dark and shapeless. She was standing against a wall with a short woman who apparently had no teeth. "She mamma," he said, pointing to the woman. "She die in two camp."

"Mr. Guizac," Mrs. McIntyre said, pushing the picture back at him, "I will not have my niggers upset. I cannot run this place without my niggers. I can run it without you but not without them and if you mention this girl to Sulk again, you won't have a job with me. Do you understand?" His face showed no comprehension. He seemed to be piecing all these words together in his mind to make a thought.

Mrs. McIntyre remembered Mrs. Shortley's words: "He understands everything, he only pretends he don't so as to do exactly as he pleases," and her face regained the look of shocked wrath she had begun with. "I cannot understand how a man who calls himself a Christian," she said, "could bring a poor innocent girl over here and marry her to something like that. I cannot understand it. I cannot!" and she shook her head and looked into the distance with a pained blue gaze.

After a second he shrugged and let his arms drop as if he were tired. "She no care black," he said. "She in camp three year."

Mrs. McIntyre felt a peculiar weakness behind her knees. "Mr. Guizac," she said, "I don't want to have to speak to you about this again. If I do, you'll have to find another place yourself. Do you understand?"

The patched face did not say. She had the impression that he didn't see her there. "This is my place," she said. "I say who will come here and who won't."

"Ya," he said and put back on his cap.

"I am not responsible for the world's misery," she said as an afterthought.

"Ya," he said.

"You have a good job. You should be grateful to be here," she added, "but I'm not sure you are."

"Ya," he said and gave his little shrug and turned back to the tractor.

She watched him get on and maneuver the machine into the corn again. When he had passed her and rounded the turn, she climbed to the top of the slope and stood with her arms folded and looked out grimly over the field. "They're all the same," she muttered, "whether they come from Poland or Tennessee. I've handled Herrins and Ringfields and Shortleys and I can handle a Guizac," and she narrowed her gaze until it closed entirely around the diminishing figure on the tractor as if she were watching him through a gunsight. All her life she had been fighting the world's overflow and now she had it in the form of a Pole. "You're 'Just like all the rest of them she said, "-only smart and thrifty and energetic but so am I. And this is my place," and she stood there, a small black-hatted, black-smocked figure with an aging cherubic face, and folded her arms as if she were equal to anything. But her heart was beating as if some interior violence had already been done to her. She opened her eyes to include the whole field so that the figure on the tractor was no larger than a grasshopper in her widened view.

She stood there for some time. There was a slight breeze and the corn trembled in great waves on both sides of the slope. The big cutter, with its monotonous roar, continued to shoot it pulverized into the wagon in a steady spurt of fodder. By nightfall, the Displaced Person would have worked his way around and around until there would be nothing on either side of the two hills but the stubble, and down in the center, risen like a little island, the graveyard where the Judge lay grinning under his desecrated monument.

Answer *true* or *false* for each of the following statements.

1.58 _____ The old black man observes that the Displaced Person is different from all of the other people who have worked for Mrs. McIntyre.

1.59 _____ One of the Judge's favorite sayings was, "The devil you know is better than the devil you don't."

1.60 _____ The Judge was buried in his family's graveyard on the farm.

1.61 _____ Mr. Guizac gives a picture of his cousin to Sulk, promising her hand in marriage if he pays for her trip to America.

1.62 _____ Mrs. McIntyre was sure that she was the richest woman in the world.

1.63 _____ Mrs. McIntyre calls Mr. Guizac a saint for attempting to marry his cousin to Sulk.

1.64 _____ The Judge concludes that the Displaced Person is ungrateful.

Section 3 — The Displaced Person

The priest, with his long bland face supported on one finger, had been talking for ten minutes about Purgatory while Mrs. McIntyre squinted furiously at him from an opposite chair. They were drinking ginger ale on her front porch and she kept rattling the ice in her glass, rattling her beads, rattling her bracelet like an impatient pony jingling its harness. There is no moral obligation to keep him, she was saying under her breath, there is absolutely no moral obligation. Suddenly she lurched up and her voice fell across his brogue like a drill into a mechanical saw. "Listen," she said, "I'm not theological. I'm practical! I want to talk to you about something practical!"

"Arrrrrrr," he groaned, grating to a halt.

She had put at least a finger of whiskey in her own ginger ale so that she would be able to endure his full-length visit and she sat down awkwardly, finding the chair closer to her than she had expected. "Mr. Guizac is not satisfactory," she said.

The old man raised his eyebrows in mock wonder.

"He's extra," she said. "He doesn't fit in. I have to have somebody who fits in."

The priest carefully turned his hat on his knees. He had a little trick of waiting a second silently and then swinging the conversation back into his own paths. He was about eighty. She had never known a priest until she had gone to see this one on the business of getting her the Displaced Person. After he had got her the Pole, he had used the business introduction to try to convert her-just as she had supposed he would.

"Give him time," the old man said. "He'll learn to fit in. Where is that beautiful birrrrd of yours?" he asked and then said, "Arrrrr, I see him!" and stood up and looked out over the lawn where the peacock and the two hens were stepping at a strained attention, their long necks ruffled, the cock's violent blue and the hens' silvergreen, glinting in the late afternoon sun.

"Mr. Guizac," Mrs. McIntyre continued, bearing down with a flat steady voice, "is very efficient. I'll admit that. But he doesn't understand how to get on with my niggers and they don't like him. I can't have my niggers run off. And I don't like his attitude. He's not the least grateful for being here."

The priest had his hand on the screen door and he opened it, ready to make his escape. "Arrrr, I must be off," he murmured.

"I tell you if I had a white man who understood the Negroes, I'd have to let Mr. Guizac go," she said and stood up again.

He turned then and looked her in the face. "He has nowhere to go," he said. Then he said, "Dear lady, I know you well enough to know you wouldn't turn him out for a trifle!" and without waiting for an answer, he raised his hand and gave her his blessing in a rumbling voice.

She smiled angrily and said, "I didn't create this situation, of course."

The priest let his eyes wander toward the birds. They had reached the middle of the lawn. The cock stopped suddenly and curving his neck backwards, he raised his tail and spread it with a shimmering timbrous noise. Tiers of small pregnant suns floated in a green-gold haze over his head. The priest stood transfixed, his jaw slack. Mrs. McIntyre wondered where she had ever seen such an idiotic old man. "Christ will come like that!" he said in a loud gay voice and wiped his hand over his mouth and stood there, gaping.

Mrs. McIntyre's face assumed a set puritanical expression and she reddened. Christ in the conversation embarrassed her the way sex had her mother. "It is not my responsibility that Mr. Guizac has nowhere to go," she said. "I don't find myself responsible for all the extra people in the world."

The old man didn't seem to hear her. His attention was fixed on the cock who was taking minute steps backward, his head against the spread tail. "The Transfiguration," he murmured.

She had no idea what he was talking about. "Mr. Guizac didn't have to come here in the first place," she said, giving him a hard look.

The cock lowered his tail and began to pick grass.

"He didn't have to come in the first place," she repeated, emphasizing each word.

The old man smiled absently. "He came to redeem us," he said and blandly reached for her hand and shook it and said he must go.

If Mr. Shortley had not returned a few weeks later, she would have gone out looking for a new man to hire. She had not wanted him back but when she saw the familiar black automobile drive up the road and stop by the side of the house, she had the feeling that she was the one returning, after a long miserable trip, to her own place. She realized all at once that it was Mrs. Shortley she had been missing. She had had no one to talk to since Mrs. Shortley left, and she ran to the door, expecting to see her heaving herself up the steps. Mr. Shortley stood there alone. He had on a black felt hat and a shirt with red and blue palm trees designed in it but the hollows in his long bitten blistered face were deeper than they had been a month ago.

"Well!" she said. "Where is Mrs. Shortley?"

Mr. Shortley didn't say anything. The change in his face seemed to have come from the inside; he looked like a man who had gone for a long time without water. "She was God's own angel," he said in a loud voice. "She was the sweetest woman in the world."

"Where is she?" Mrs. McIntyre murmured.

"Daid," he said. "She had herself a stroke on the day she left out of here." There was a corpse-like composure about his face. "I figure that Pole killed her," he said. "She seen through him from the first. She known he come from the devil. She told me so."

It took Mrs. McIntyre three days to get over Mrs. Shortley's death. She told herself that anyone would have thought they were kin. She rehired Mr. Shortley to do farm work though actually she didn't want him without his wife. She told him she was going to give thirty days' notice to the Displaced Person at the end of the month and that then he could have his job back in the dairy. Mr. Shortley preferred the dairy job but he was willing to wait. He said it would give him some satisfaction to see the Pole leave the place, and Mrs. McIntyre said it would give her a great deal of satisfaction. She confessed that she should have been content with the help she had in the first place and not have been reaching into other parts of the world for it. Mr. Shortley said he never had cared for foreigners since he had been in the first world's war and seen what they were like. He said he had seen all kinds then but that none of them were like us. He said he recalled the face of one man who had thrown a hand-grenade at him and that the man had had little round eyeglasses exactly like Mr. Guizac's.

"But Mr. Guizac is a Pole, he's not a German," Mrs. McIntyre said.

30

"It ain't a great deal of difference in them two kinds," Mr. Shortley had explained.

The Negroes were pleased to see Mr. Shortley back. The Displaced Person had expected them to work as hard as he worked himself, whereas Mr. Shortley recognized their limitations. He had never been a very good worker himself with Mrs. Shortley to keep him in line, but without her, he was even more forgetful and slow. The Pole worked as fiercely as ever and seemed to have no inkling that he was about to be fired. Mrs. McIntyre saw jobs done in a short time that she had thought would never get done at all. Still she was resolved to get rid of him. The sight of his small stiff figure moving quickly here and there had come to be the most irritating sight on the place for her, and she felt she had been tricked by the old priest. He had said there was no legal obligation for her to keep the Displaced Person if he was not satisfactory, but then he had brought up the moral one.

She meant to tell him that *her* moral obligation was to her own people, to Mr. Shortley, who had fought in the world war for his country and not to Mr. Guizac who had merely arrived here to take advantage of whatever he could. She felt she must have this out with the priest before she fired the Displaced Person. When the first of the month came and the priest hadn't called, she put off giving the Pole notice for a little longer.

Mr. Shortley told himself that he should have known all along that no woman was going to do what she said she was when she said she was. He didn't know how long he could afford to put up with her shilly-shallying. He thought himself that she was going soft and was afraid to turn the Pole out for fear he would have a hard time getting another place. He could tell her the truth about this: that if she let him go, in three years he would own his own house and have a television aerial sitting on top of it. As a matter of policy, Mr. Shortley began to come to her back door every evening to put certain facts before her. "A white man sometimes don't get the consideration a nigger gets," he said, "but that don't matter because he's still white, but sometimes," and here he would pause and look off into the distance, "a man that's fought and bled and died in the service of his native land don't get the consideration of one of them like them he was fighting. I ast you: is that right?" When he asked her such questions he could watch her face and tell he was making an impression. She didn't look too well these days. He noticed lines around her eyes that hadn't been there when he and Mrs. Shortley had been the only white help on the place. Whenever he thought of Mrs. Shortley, he felt his heart go down like an old bucket into a dry well.

The old priest kept away as if he had been frightened by his last visit but finally, seeing that the Displaced Person had not been fired, he ventured to call again to take up giving Mrs. McIntyre instructions where he remembered leaving them off. She had not asked to be instructed but he instructed anyway, forcing a little definition of one of the sacraments or of some dogma into each conversation he had, no matter with whom. He sat on her porch, taking no notice of her partly mocking, partly outraged expression as she sat shaking her foot, waiting for an opportunity to drive a wedge into his talk. "For," he was saying, as if he spoke of something that had happened yesterday in town, "when God sent his Only Begotten Son, Jesus Christ Our Lord' — he slightly bowed his head — "as a Redeemer to mankind, He..."

"Father Flynn!" she said in a voice that made him jump. "I want to talk to you about something serious!"

The skin under the old man's right eye flinched.

"As far as I'm concerned," she said and glared at him fiercely, "Christ was just another D.P."

He raised his hands slightly and let them drop on his knees. "Arrrrrr," he murmured as if he were considering this.

"I'm going to let that man go," she said. "I don't have any obligation to him. My obligation is to the people who've done something for their country, not to the ones who've just come over to take advantage of what they can get," and she began to talk rapidly, remembering all her arguments. The priest's attention seemed to retire to some private oratory to wait until she got through. Once or twice his gaze roved out onto the lawn as if he were hunting some means of escape but she didn't stop. She told him how she had been hanging onto this place for thirty years, always just barely making it against people who came from nowhere and were going nowhere, who didn't want anything but an automobile. She said she had found out they were the same whether they came from Poland or Tennessee. When the Guizacs got ready, she said, they would not hesitate to leave her. She told him how the people who looked rich were the poorest of all because they had the most to keep up. She asked him how he thought she paid her feed bills. She told him she would like to have her house done over but she couldn't afford it. She couldn't even afford to have the monument restored over her husband's grave. She asked him if he would like to guess what her insurance amounted to for the year. Finally she asked him if he thought she was made of money and the old man suddenly let out a great ugly bellow as if this were a comical question.

When the visit was over, she felt let down, though she had clearly triumphed over him. She made up her mind now that on the first of the month, she would give the Displaced Person his thirty days' notice and she told Mr. Shortley so.

Mr. Shortley didn't say anything. His wife had been the only woman he was ever acquainted with who was never scared off from doing what she said. She said the Pole had been sent by the devil and the priest. Mr. Shortley had no doubt that the priest had got some peculiar control over Mrs. McIntyre and that before long she would start attending his Masses. She looked as if something was wearing her down from the inside. She was thinner and more fidgety, and not as sharp as she used to be. She would look at a milk can now and not see how dirty it was and he had seen her lips move when she was not talking. The Pole never did anything the wrong way but all the same he was very irritating to her. Mr. Shortley himself did things as he pleased—not always her way—but she didn't seem to notice. She had noticed though that the Pole and all his family were getting fat; she pointed out to Mr. Shortley that the hollows had come out of their cheeks and that they saved every cent they made. "Yes'm, and one of these days he'll be able to buy and sell you out," Mr. Shortley had ventured to say, and he could tell that the statement had shaken her.

"I'm just waiting for the first," she had said.

Mr. Shortley waited too and the first came and went and she didn't fire him. He could have told anybody how it would be. He was not a violent man but he hated to see a woman done in by a foreigner. He felt that that was one thing a man couldn't stand by and see happen.

There was no reason Mrs. McIntyre should not fire Mr. Guizac at once but she put it off from day to day. She was worried about her bills and about her health. She didn't sleep at night or when she did she dreamed about the Displaced Person. She had never discharged anyone before; they had all left her. One night she dreamed that Mr. Guizac and his family were moving into her house and that she was moving in with Mr. Shortley. This was too much for her and she woke up and didn't sleep again for several nights; and one night she dreamed that the priest came to call and droned on and on saying,

32

"Dear lady, I know your tender heart won't suffer you to turn the porrrrr man out. Think of the thousands of them, think of the ovens and the boxcars and the camps and the sick children and Christ Our Lord."

"He's extra and he's upset the balance around here," she said, "and I'm a logical practical woman and there are no ovens here and no camps and no Christ Our Lord and when he leaves, he'll make more money. He'll work at the mill and buy a car and don't talk to me-all they want is a car."

"The ovens and the boxcars and the sick children," droned the priest, "and our dear Lord."

"Just one too many," she said.

The next morning, she made up her mind while she was eating her breakfast that she would give him his notice at once, and she stood up and walked out of the kitchen and down the road with her table napkin still in her hand. Mr. Guizac was spraying the barn, standing in his swaybacked way with one hand on his hip. He turned off the hose and gave her an impatient kind of attention as if she were interfering with his work. She had not thought of what she would say to him, she had merely come. She stood in the barn door, looking severely at the wet spotless floor and the dripping stanchions. "Ya goot?" he said.

"Mr. Guizac," she said, "I can barely meet my obligations now." Then she said in a louder, stronger voice, emphasizing each word, "I have bills to pay."

"I too," Mr. Guizac said. "Much bills, little money," and he shrugged.

At the other end of the barn, she saw a long beak-nosed shadow glide like a snake halfway up the sunlit open door and stop; and somewhere behind her, she was aware of a silence where the sound of the Negroes shoveling had come a minute before. "This is my place," she said angrily. "All of you are extra. Each and every one of you are extra!"

"Ya," Mr. Guizac said and turned on the hose again.

She wiped her mouth with the napkin she had in her hand and walked off, as if she had accomplished what she came for.

Mr. Shortley's shadow withdrew from the door and he leaned against the side of the barn and lit half of a cigarette that he took out of his pocket. There was nothing for him to do now but wait on the hand of God to strike, but he knew one thing: he was not going to wait with his mouth shut.

Starting that morning, he began to complain and to state his side of the case to every person he saw, black or white. He complained in the grocery store and at the courthouse and on the street corner and directly to Mrs. McIntyre herself, for there was nothing underhanded about him. If the Pole could have understood what he had to say, he would have said it to him too. "All men was created free and equal," he said to Mrs. McIntyre, "and I risked my life and limb to prove it. Gone over there and fought and bled and died and come back on over here and find out who's got my job—just exactly who I been fighting. It was a hand-grenade come that near to killing me and I seen who throwed it-little man with eye-glasses just like his. Might have bought them at the same store. Small world," and he gave a bitter little laugh. Since he didn't have Mrs. Shortley to do the talking any more, he had started doing it himself and had found that he had a gift for it. He had the power of making other people see his logic. He talked a good deal to the Negroes.

"Whyn't you go back to Africa?" he asked Sulk one morning as they were cleaning out the silo. "That's your country, ain't it?"

"I ain't goin there," the boy said. "They might eat me up."

"Well, if you behave yourself it isn't any reason you can't stay here," Mr. Shortley said kindly. "Because you didn't run away from nowhere. Your granddaddy was bought. He didn't have a thing to do with coming. It's the people that run away from where they come from that I ain't got any use for."

"I never felt no need to travel," the Negro said.

"Well," Mr. Shortley said, "if I was going to travel again, it would be to either China or Africa. You go to either of them two places and you can tell right away what the difference is between you and them. You go to these other places and the only way you can tell is if they say something. And then you can't always tell because about half of them know the English language. That's where we make our mistake," he said, "—letting all them people onto English. There'd be a heap less trouble if everybody only knew his own language. My wife said knowing two languages was like having eyes in the back of your head. You couldn't put nothing over on her."

"YOU sho couldn't," the boy muttered, and then be added, "She was fine. She was sho fine. I never known a finer white woman than her."

Mr. Shortley turned in the opposite direction and worked silently for a while. After a few minutes he leaned up and tapped the colored boy on the shoulder with the handle of his shovel. For a second he only looked at him while a great deal of meaning gathered in his wet eyes. Then be said softly, "Revenge is mine, saith the Lord."

Mrs. McIntyre found that everybody in town knew Mr. Shortley's version of her business and that everyone was critical of her conduct. She began to understand that she had a moral obligation to fire the Pole and that she was shirking it because she found it hard to do. She could not stand the increasing guilt any longer and on a cold Saturday morning, she started off after breakfast to fire him. She walked down to the machine shed where she heard him cranking up the tractor.

There was a heavy frost on the ground that made the fields look like the rough backs of sheep; the sun was almost silver and the woods stuck up like dry bristles on the sky line. The countryside seemed to be receding from the little circle of noise around the shed. Mr. Guizac was squatting on the ground beside the small tractor, putting in a part. Mrs. McIntyre hoped to get the fields turned over while he still had thirty days to work for her. The colored boy was standing by with some tools in his hand and Mr. Shortley was under the shed about to get up on the large tractor and back it out. She meant to wait until he and the Negro got out of the way before she began her unpleasant duty.

She stood watching Mr. Guizac, stamping her feet on the hard ground, for the cold was climbing like a paralysis up her feet and legs. She had on a heavy black coat and a red head-kerchief with her black hat pulled down on top of it to keep the glare out of her eyes. Under the black brim her face had an abstracted look and once or twice her lips moved silently. Mr. Guizac shouted over the noise of the tractor for the Negro to hand him a screwdriver and when he got it, he turned over on his back on the icy ground and reached up under the machine. She could not see his face, only his feet and legs and trunk sticking impudently out from the side of the tractor. He had on rubber boots that were cracked and splashed with mud. He raised one knee and then lowered it and turned himself slightly. Of all the things she resented about him, she resented most that he hadn't left on his own accord.

Mr. Shortley had got on the large tractor and was backing it out from under the shed. He seemed to be warmed by it as if its heat and strength sent impulses

34

up through him that he obeyed instantly. He had headed it toward the small tractor but he braked it on a slight incline and jumped off and turned back toward the shed. Mrs. McIntyre was looking fixedly at Mr. Guizac's legs lying flat on the ground now. She heard the brake on the large tractor slip and, looking up, she saw it move forward, calculating its own path. Later she remembered that she had seen the Negro jump silently out of the way as if a spring in the earth had released him and that she had seen Mr. Shortley turn his head with incredible slowness and stare silently over his shoulder and that she had started to shout to the Displaced Person but that she had not. She had felt her eyes and Mr. Shortley's eyes and the Negro's eyes come together in one took that froze them in collusion forever, and she had heard the little noise the Pole made as the tractor wheel broke his backbone. The two men ran forward to help and she fainted.

She remembered, when she came to, running somewhere, perhaps into the house and out again but she could not remember what for or if she had fainted again when she got there. When she finally came back to where the tractors were, the ambulance had arrived. Mr. Guizac's body was covered with the bent bodies of his wife and two children and by a black one which hung over him, murmuring words she didn't understand. At first she thought this must be the doctor but then with a feeling of annoyance she recognized the priest, who had come with the ambulance and was slipping something into the crushed man's mouth. After a minute he stood up and she looked first at his bloody pants legs and then at his face which was not averted from her but was as withdrawn and expressionless as the rest of the countryside. She only stared at him for she was too shocked by her experience to be quite herself. Her mind was not taking hold of all that was happening. She felt she was in some foreign country where the people bent over the body were natives, and she watched like a stranger while the dead man was carried away in the ambulance.

That evening, Mr. Shortley left without notice to look for a new position and the Negro, Sulk, was taken with a sudden desire to see more of the world and set off for the southern part of the state. The old man Astor could not work without company. Mrs. McIntyre hardly noticed that she had no help left for she came down with a nervous affliction and had to go to the hospital. When she came back, she saw that the place would be too much for her to run now and she turned her cows over to a professional auctioneer (who sold them at a loss) and retired to live on what she had, while she tried to save her declining health. A numbness developed in one of her legs and her bands and head began to jiggle and eventually she had to stay in bed all the time with only a colored woman to wait on her. Her eyesight grew steadily worse and she lost her voice altogether. Not many people remembered to come out to the country to see her except the old priest. He came regularly once a week with a bag of breadcrumbs and, after be had fed these to the peacock, he would come in and sit by the side of her bed and explain the doctrines of the Church.

Answer _true_ or _false_ for each of the following statements.

1.65   _____   The priest declares that he is not theological but practical.

1.66   _____   Mrs. McIntyre tells the priest that Mr. Guizac is not satisfactory and that she is not responsible for all of the extra people in the world.

1.67   _____   While looking at the peacock's beauty, the priest is reminded of Christ.

1.68   _____   The priest tells Mrs. McIntyre that she has a moral duty to Mr. Guizac.

1.69   _____   Mr. Shortley blames Mrs. Shortley's death on her own temper.

1.70   _____   Mrs. McIntyre believes that "Christ was just another D. P."

35

1.71   _____   Even though Mr. Guizac never did anything wrong to Mrs. McIntyre, he was nevertheless irritating to her.

1.72   _____   The thing about Mr. Guizac that Mrs. McIntyre resented the most was that he never left of his own accord.

1.73   _____   When the tractor started to roll toward Mr. Guizac, Sulk, Mrs. McIntyre, and Mr. Shortley did everything they could to stop it from killing him.

1.74   _____   The old priest is the only person who comes out to visit Mrs. McIntyre after she becomes bedridden.

Theodore Roethke (1908–1963). Theodore Roethke instructed his beginning students to imitate poets of the past, to "write like someone else." He "shunned undisciplined and formless" means of expression. Instead, he valued traditional forms of rhythm and meter, finding within them a freedom to express himself in a most intensely beautiful way.

Roethke was the son and grandson of commercial greenhouse owners. Under the "godlike" care of his father, the greenhouses were a place of both anxiety and wonder to Roethke. In his childhood he was surrounded by the growth and death of nature, which became the source of many of his poems.

Educated at the University of Michigan and Harvard, he began his lifelong career in teaching at Lafayette College in 1931. In 1941 he published his first book, *Open House*. Great change occurred between this first volume and his last, *The Far Field*, which was published posthumously in 1964. He was a man with mental problems and an alcohol dependency; therefore, his work swung from expressions of anxiety and hate to poems of love and pleasure. As a collective whole, his work has been viewed as a journey of the soul, a spiritual quest for peace and understanding; however, apart from God's revelation, he did not find it. In 1954 he won the Pulitzer Prize for Poetry and is acclaimed as one of America's leading poets.

Fill in each of the blanks using items from the following word list.

childhood   traditional   formless
greenhouses   peace

1.75   Theodore Roethke shunned undisciplined and _____ means of expression.

1.76   He valued _____ forms of poetry.

1.77   Roethke's father owned and operated commercial _____ .

1.78   Roethke's _____ is the source of many of his poems.

1.79   Roethke's poems are a reflection of his spiritual quest for _____ and understanding.

What to Look For:

Like the Imagists before him, Theodore Roethke used concrete images to evoke emotion. However, his poetry does try to communicate wisdom to the reader. As you read the following selection, pay close attention to the concrete images. How do the images "bring to life" what the speaker is saying?

Root Cellar

Nothing would sleep in that cellar, dank as a ditch,
Bulbs broke out of boxes hunting for chinks* in the dark,
Shoots dangled and drooped,
Lolloing obscenely from mildewed crates,
Hung down long evil necks, like tropical snakes.   5
And what a congress* of stinks—
Roots as ripe as old bait,
Pulpy stems, rank, silo-rich,
Leaf-mold, manure, lime, piled against slippery planks.
Nothing would give up life:.   10
Even the dirt kept breathing a small breath.

"Root Cellar", copyright © 1943 by Modern Poetry Association, Inc. from THE COLLECTED POEMS OF THEODORE ROETHKE by Theodore Roethke. Used by permission of Doubleday, a division of Random House, Inc.

One of Roethke's famous "greenhouse poems," it speaks of man's attempt to control life. But as the poem concludes, this is futile. Job 12:10 states that the life of every living thing is in the hand of the Lord.

chinks - any bit of light
congress - a collection

 Fill in each of the blanks using items from the following word list.

pulpy	ditch	futile
yellow	light	breathing
necks	nothing	snakes
ripe		

1.80   The poem is about man's _____ attempt to control life.

1.81   The cellar is as dank as a _____ .

1.82   According to line 2, the bulbs are hunting for _____ .

1.83   According to lines 3–5, the shoots look like _____ with _____ evil _____ .

1.84   Far from dead, the roots are _____ and the stems are _____ .

1.85   According to line 10, despite being in the cellar, _____ would die.

1.86   According to line 11, even dirt—a seemingly lifeless thing—kept _____ .

 Review the material in this section in preparation for the Self-Test, which will check your mastery of this particular section. The items missed on this Self-Test will indicate specific areas where restudy is necessary for mastery.

SELF-TEST 1

Underline the correct answer in each of the following statements (each answer, 2 points).

1.01   The (medieval, modern, postmodern) age began with the French Revolution.

1.02   The French Revolution exalted (human reason, divine revelation, the Bible).

1.03   (Communism, Capitalism, Democracy) is the most thoroughgoing attempt to remake society by means of human reason.

1.04   The Iron Curtain limited the citizens of (democratic, communist, socialist) states from relations with Western Europe and the United States.

1.05   The Modern Age searched for truth apart from (Christianity, communism, Marxism).

1.06   The (1930s, 1920s, 1950s) were characterized by economic success, technological advances, and social stability.

1.07   During the 1950s, people came to trust (religion, society, technology) without reservation.

1.08   In the technological age, the (television, Bible, reason of man) became the great authenticator of truth.

1.09   The (1950s, 1960s, 1990s) encouraged a rapid decline in morals and the rejection of absolute truth.

1.010 After the 1960s, God and objective truth were removed from (Christian, African-American, popular) culture.

1.011 (Christianity, Marxism, Existentialism) is the belief that people have absolute freedom of choice.

1.012 An absolute truth is (always, sometimes, occasionally) true.

1.013 Existentialism is directly opposed to (Marxist, democratic, Christian) thought.

1.014 (God, Man, Government) alone is the author of truth.

1.015 Flannery O'Connor's stories paint a realistic picture of man's (sinfulness, purity, beauty).

1.016 Flannery O'Connor believed that at the center of the meaning of life was the redemption that is provided by (man, society, Christ).

Fill in each of the blanks using items from the following word list (each answer, 2 points).

valued	breathing	childhood
formless	futile	universal
grotesque	morals	nothing
peace	poetry	social
stream-of-consciousness	traditional	similar
society	blurred	God

1.017 The rise and fall of the Tower of Babel and modernism are _____ .

1.018 In postmodern society, a _____ standard of truth no longer exists.

1.019 American literature reflects the shifts in _____ .

1.020 Societies that stop believing in a universal standard of _____ tend to lose their ability to create great pieces of art.

1.021 American culture has moved away from the deep truths of _____ .

38

1.022   Novels and short stories of the postmodern era show elements of _____ works.

1.023   Blending nonfiction and fiction creates a _____ sense of reality.

1.024   The _____ technique continues to be used in postmodern writing.

1.025   Fiction writers from the South have produced works that have been called _____ .

1.026   The most popular _____ to emerge during the postmodern era has been written in traditional form.

1.027   The works of black writers reflected a need for _____ change.

1.028   Theodore Roethke shunned undisciplined and _____ means of expression.

1.029   Roethke _____ traditional forms of poetry.

1.030   Roethke's _____ is the source of many of his poems.

1.031   Roethke's poems are a reflection of his spiritual quest for _____ and understanding.

1.032   Roethke's poem "Root Cellar" is about man's _____ attempt to control life.

1.033   According to line 10 of the "Root Cellar," despite being in the cellar, _____ would die.

1.034   According to line 11 of the "Root Cellar," even dirt — a seemingly lifeless thing — kept _____ .

Answer *true* or *false* for each of the following statements (each answer, 2 points).

1.035   _____   The mayor brought the Displaced Person and his family to Mrs. McIntyre's farm.

1.036   _____   The Guizacs are from a foreign country.

1.037   _____   Mrs. Shortley, seeing Mr. Guizac's desire to work hard, declared, "That man is my salvation!"

1.038   _____   Mrs. Shortley believed that Mr. Guizac was from the devil.

1.039   _____   The old black man observes that the Displaced Person is different from all the other people who have worked for Mrs. McIntyre.

1.040   _____   Mrs. McIntyre calls Mr. Guizac a saint for attempting to marry his cousin to Sulk.

1.041   _____   The priest declares that he is not theological but practical.

1.042   _____   Mrs. McIntyre tells the priest that Mr. Guizac is not satisfactory and that she is not responsible for all of the extra people in the world.

1.043   _____   While looking at the peacock's beauty, the priest is reminded of Christ.

1.044   _____   Mr. Shortley blames Mrs. Shortley's death on her own temper.

1.045   _____   Mrs. McIntyre believes that "Christ was just another D. P."

1.046   _____   The thing about Mr. Guizac that Mrs. McIntyre resented the most was that he never left of his own accord.

1.047 _____ When the tractor started to roll toward Mr. Guizac, Sulk, Mrs. McIntyre, and Mr. Shortley did everything they could to stop it from killing him.

1.048 _____ The old priest is the only person who comes out to visit Mrs. McIntyre after she becomes bedridden.

For Thought and Discussion:

Describe to a parent/teacher the characters in Flannery O'Connor's short story "The Displaced Person." Be sure to comment on the words and actions of Mrs. McIntyre, Mr. and Mrs. Shortley, the priest, and Mr. Guizac. In light of 1 John 3:7–18, discuss which characters are the children of the devil and which are the children of God. Or which characters are grotesque and which appear like Christ?

Score _____

Teacher check _____

                 Initial   Date

AMERICAN LITERATURE

LIFEPAC TEST

82/102

Name _____

Date _____

Score _____

AMERICAN LITERATURE LIFEPAC FIVE TEST

Underline the correct answer in each of the following statements (each answer, 1 point).

1. In postmodern society, a universal standard of (dress, truth, laws) no longer exists.

2. Societies that stop believing in a universal standard of morals tend to (regain, lose, enhance) their ability to create great pieces of art.

3. Fiction writers from the South have produced works that have been called (lovely, beautiful, grotesque).

4. Novels and short stories of the (premodern, postmodern, modern) era show elements of traditional works.

5. The (stream-of-consciousness, television, social) technique continues to be used in postmodern writing.

6. Roethke (despised, hated, valued) traditional forms of poetry.

7. The works of black writers reflect a need for (religious, personal, social) change.

8. Roethke's poems are a reflection of his spiritual quest for (peace, turmoil, pain) and understanding.

9. According to line 11 of Roethke's poem the "Root Cellar," even dirt—a seemingly lifeless thing—kept (dying, breathing, coughing).

10. John Updike focuses upon the everyday life of the (upper, lower, middle) class.

11. Updike's stories diagnose (societal, medical, valued) and personal ills while offering a religious and moral cure.

12. Dr. Martin Luther King Jr. adopted the nonviolent protest philosophy of (Gandhi, John F. Kennedy, Thomas Paine).

13. Dr. Martin Luther King Jr. often compared himself to (James, Moses, Abraham) and his people's difficulties to ancient Israel's enslavement in (Egypt, Chicago, Iraq).

14. Chicago and its black society are the subject matter of much of Gwendolyn Brooks's (lectures, poetry, paintings).

15. Brooks's most recent work reflects a push toward black community and (shame, pride, humility).

16. Much of Brooks's poetry is written in (modern, traditional, progressive) form.

17. The most popular (poetry, fiction, nonfiction) to emerge during the postmodern era has been written in traditional form.

Answer *true* or *false* for each of the following statements (each answer, 3 points).

18. _____ In the short story, "The Displaced Person," Mrs. Shortley believed that Mr. Guizac was an angel sent from God.

19. _____ Mr. Guizac believed that "Christ was just another D. P."

20. _____ The Guizacs were from Chicago.

21. _____ Mrs. McIntyre declares that she is not theological but practical.

22. _____ In Eudora Welty's short story "A Worn Path," Phoenix Jackson makes the long journey to get medicine for herself.

23. _____ In Updike's short story "Separating," Judith was most nearly Richard's conscience.

24. _____ Martin Luther King Jr. had a dream that one day the nation would live out the true meaning of its creed: "We hold these truths to be self-evident, that all men are created equal."

25. _____ Martin Luther King quoted two songs in his "I Have a Dream" speech: a white hymn and "Freedom."

26. _____ In Ellison's book *Invisible Man*, the speaker says that he is an invisible man because he goes out only at night.

27. _____ The blonde man and the invisible man become confused over the meaning of freedom.

28. _____ The invisible man takes responsibility for the near murder and surrenders himself to the police.

29. _____ According to line 5 of Brooks's poem "Lovers of the Poor," the ladies have humble faces.

30. _____ In "Lovers of the Poor," the ladies want to give to only the "worthy poor."

31. _____ According to lines 90–92, the ladies refuse to give their "loathe-love" because the people have no need of their money.

Fill in each of the blanks using items from the following word list (each answer, 3 points).

snapshot	change	television
Christian	writer	God
Existentialism	facts	Americans
sinfulness	human reason	Christianity
modern	South	

32. Eudora Welty's stories capture the details of life in the deep _____.

33. The Modern Age searched for truth apart from _____.

34. The French Revolution exalted _____.

35. _____ is the belief that people have unlimited freedom of choice.

36. _____ alone is the author of truth.

37. In the technological age, the _____ became the great authenticator of truth.

38. Existentialism is directly opposed to _____ thought.

39. The _____ age began with the French Revolution.

40. Robert Lowell's poetry is marked by public and personal _____ .

41. Flannery O'Connor's stories paint a realistic picture of man's _____ .

42. Frustrated, the speaker in Lowell's poem "Epilogue" says that his work is like a
_____ .

43. According to line 20 of Lowell's poem "Epilogue," people are "poor passing
_____ ."

44. Ellison has proclaimed himself to be a _____ rather than a spokesman.

45. *Invisible Man* is about all _____ and their search for self and being.

Thinking and Writing

Choose one of the following "Thought and Discussion" topics.
Write your answer on a separate piece of paper.

1. Explain John Updike's short story *Separating*. Be sure to mention the apparent happiness of the parents. In light of Jesus' provisions for divorce as stated in Matt 19:8–9, discuss the validity of Richard and Joan's separation. Why is Dickie's question "Why?" so piercing to Richard's conscience? How is Richard and Joan's situation typical of many couples today?

2. Explain the purpose and content of Dr. Martin Luther King's "I Have a Dream" speech. Be sure to comment on his use of the Declaration of Independence, the U. S. Constitution, and the Christian concept of brotherhood to support the civil rights movement. In light of Colossians 3:11, discuss the connection between Christianity and the equality of all men. How has the Christian belief in the equality of men played an important part in the civil rights movement?

3. Describe the words and actions of Mrs. McIntyre, Mr. and Mrs. Shortley, the priest, and Mr. Guizac in Flannery O'Connor's short story "The Displaced Person." In light of 1 John 3:7–18, discuss which characters are the children of the devil and which are the children of God. Or which characters are grotesque and which appear like Christ?

II. MORE CONTEMPORARY WRITERS

Eudora Welty (1909–2001). Described before her death as "America's foremost living woman writer of fiction," Eudora Welty captured with compassion the details of life in the Deep South. She was a life-long resident of Mississippi.

Welty's rise to prominence grew out of her experiences as a government photographer during the Depression. The job required her to record the poverty of her state, bringing her close to the struggles and hardships of poor rural areas. Moved by what she saw through her camera lens, Welty began writing, creating powerful word pictures of the Mississippi delta. Her characters are often painted with the detail and depth of a black and white photograph. Unlike many of the other writers of her time, a sense of optimism always pervades her stories.

In 1936 a small magazine published Welty's first short story, "Death of a Traveling Salesman." From that point, Welty found success as both a short story writer and a novelist. A collection of her short stories was first published in 1941 as *A Curtain of Green*. She went on to publish several volumes of short stories. In 1973 she won the Pulitzer Prize for her novel *The Optimist's Daughter* (1972). Her other novels include *Delta Wedding* (1946) and *The Ponder Heart* (1954).

 Underline the correct answer in each of the following statements.

2.1   Eudora Welty was described as "America's foremost living woman writer of (poetry, fiction, nonfiction)."

2.2   During the Depression, Welty worked as a government (agent, photographer, writer).

2.3   Welty's stories capture the details of life in the Deep (North, South, West).

2.4   Welty is a successful short story writer and (poet, governor, novelist).

2.5   In 1973 she won the (Pulitzer, Bollingen, Nobel) Prize for her novel *The Optimist's Daughter*.

2.6   Welty was a life-long resident of (Missouri, New York City, Mississippi).

What to Look For:

The main character of the following story is Phoenix Jackson. Her name has significance. The phoenix is a bird from Greek mythology that symbolizes immortality. After being burned by fire, it resurrects itself. Jackson is the name of the capital of Mississippi and of two Southern generals during the Civil War. As you read, think about Phoenix Jackson's name. How do the details of Phoenix's character paint a powerful picture of enduring devotion. What is significant about the fact that she is black and poor?

"A Worn Path"

It was December — a bright frozen day in the early morning. Far out in the country there was an old Negro woman with her head tied red rag, coming along a path through the pinewoods. Her name was Phoenix Jackson. She was very old and small and she walked slowly in the dark pine shadows, moving a little from side to side in her steps, with the balanced heaviness and lightness of a pendulum in a grandfather clock. She carried a thin, small cane made from an umbrella, and with this she kept tapping the frozen earth in front of her. This made a grave and persistent noise in the still air, that seemed meditative, like the chirping of a solitary little bird.

She wore a dark striped dress reaching down to her shoe tops, and an equally long apron of bleached sugar sacks, with a full pocket: all neat and tidy, but every time she took a step she might have fallen over her shoelaces, which dragged from her unlaced shoes. She looked straight ahead. Her eyes were blue with age. Her skin had a pattern all its own of numberless branching wrinkles and as though a whole little tree stood in the middle of her forehead, but a golden color ran underneath, and the two knobs of her cheeks were illumined by a yellow burning under the dark. Under the red rag her hair came down on her neck in the frailest of ringlets, still black, and with an odor like copper.

Now and then there was a quivering in the thicket. Old Phoenix said, "Out of my way, all you foxes, owls, beetles, jack rabbits, coons and wild animals!...Keep out from under these feet, little bob-whites...Keep the big wild hogs out of my path. Don't let none of those come running my direction. I got a long way." Under her small black-freckled hand her cane, limber as a buggy whip, would switch at the brush as if to rouse up any hiding things.

On she went. The woods were deep and still. The sun made the pine needles almost too bright to look at, up where the wind rocked. The cones dropped as light as feathers. Down in the hollow was the mourning dove—it was not too late for him.

The path ran up a hill. "Seem like there is chains about my feet, time I get this far," she said, in the voice of argument old people keep to use with themselves. "Something always take a hold of me on this hill — pleads I should stay."

After she got to the top she turned and gave a full, severe look behind her where she had come. "Up through pines," she said at length. "Now down through oaks."

Her eyes opened their widest, and she started down gently. But before she got to the bottom of the hill a bush caught her dress.

Her fingers were busy and intent, but her skirts were full and long, so that before she could pull them free in one place they were caught in another. It was not possible to allow the dress to tear. "I in the thorny bush," she said. "Thorns, you doing your appointed work. Never want to let folks pass, no sir. Old eyes thought you was a pretty little green bush."

Finally, trembling all over, she stood free, and after a moment dared to stoop for her cane.

"Sun so high!" she cried, leaning back and looking, while the thick tears went over her eyes. "The time getting all gone here."

At the foot of this hill was a place where a log was laid across the creek.

"Now comes the trial," said Phoenix.

Putting her right foot out, she mounted the log and shut her eyes. Lifting her skirt, leveling her cane fiercely before her, like a festival figure in some parade, she began to march across. Then she opened her eyes and she was safe on the other side.

"I wasn't as old as I thought," she said.

But she sat down to rest. She spread her skirts on the bank around her and folded her hands over her knees. Up above her was a tree in a pearly cloud of mistletoe. She did not dare to close her eyes, and when a little boy brought her a plate with a slice of marble-cake on it she spoke to him. "That would be acceptable," she said. But when she went to take it there was just her own hand in the air.

So she left that tree, and had to go through a barbed-wire fence. There she had to creep and crawl, spreading her knees and stretching her fingers like a baby trying to climb the steps. But she talked loudly to herself: she could not let her dress be torn now, so late in the day, and she could not pay for having her arm or her leg sawed off if she got caught fast where she was.

At last she was safe through the fence and risen up out in the clearing. Big dead trees, like black men with one arm, were standing in the purple stalks of the withered cotton field. There sat a buzzard.

"Who you watching?"

In the furrow she made her way along.

"Glad this not the season for bulls," she said, looking sideways, "and the good Lord made his snakes to curl up and sleep in the winter. A pleasure I don't see no two-headed snake coming around that tree, where it come once. It took a while to get by him, back in the summer."

She passed through the old cotton and went into a field of dead corn. It whispered and shook and was taller than her head. "Through the maze now," she said, for there was no path.

Then there was something tall, black, and skinny there, moving before her.

At first she took it for a man. It could have been a man dancing in the field. But she stood still and listened, and it did not make a sound. It was as silent as a ghost.

"Ghost," she said sharply, "who be you the ghost of? For I have heard of nary death close by."

But there was no answer — only the ragged dancing in the wind.

She shut her eyes, reached out her hand, and touched a sleeve. She found a coat and inside that an emptiness, cold as ice.

"You scarecrow," she said. Her face lighted. "I ought to be shut up for good," she said with laughter. "My senses is gone. I too old. I the oldest people I ever know. Dance, old scarecrow," she said, "while I dancing with you."

She kicked her foot over the furrow, and with mouth drawn down, shook her head once or twice in a little strutting way. Some husks blew down and whirled in streamers about her skirts.

Then she went on, parting her way from side to side with the cane, through the whispering field. At last she came to the end, to a wagon track where the silver

43

glass blew between the red ruts. The quail were walking around like pullets, seeming all dainty and unseen.

"Walk pretty," she said. "This the easy place. This the easy going."

She followed the track, swaying through the quiet bare fields, through the little strings of trees silver in their dead leaves, past cabins silver from weather, with the doors and windows baorded shut, all like old women under a spell sitting there. "I walking in their sleep," she said, nodding her head vigorously.

In a ravine she went where a spring was silently flowing through a hollow log. Old Phoenix bent and drank. "Sweet-gum makes the water sweet," she said, and drank more. "Nobody know who made this well, for it was here when I was born."

The track crossed a swampy part where the moss hung as white as lace from every limb. "Sleep on, alligators, and blow your bubbles." Then the track went into the road.

Deep, deep the road went down between the high green-colored banks. Overhead the live-oaks met, and it was as dark as a cave.

A black dog with a lolling tongue came up out of the weeds by the ditch. She was meditating, and not ready, and when he came at her she only hit him a little with her cane. Over she went in the ditch, like a little puff of milkweed.

Down there, her senses drifted away. A dream visited her, and she reached her hand up, but nothing reached down and gave her a pull. So she lay there and presently went to talking. "Old woman," she said to herself, "that black dog come up out of the weeds to stall you off, and now there he sitting on his fine tail, smiling at you."

A white man finally came along and found her — a hunter, a young man, with his dog on a chain.

"Well, Granny!" he laughed. "What are you doing there?"

"Lying on my back like a June-bug waiting to be fumed over, mister," she said, reaching up her hand.

He lifted her up, gave her a swing in the air, and set her down. "Anything broken, Granny?"

"No sir, them old dead weeds is springy enough," said Phoenix, when she had got her breath. "I thank you for your trouble."

"Where do you live, Granny?" he asked, while the two dogs were growling at each other.

"Away back yonder, sir, behind the ridge. You can't even see it from here."

"On your way home?"

"No sir, I going to town."

"Why, that's too far! That's as far as I walk when I come out myself, and I get something for my trouble." He patted the stuffed bag he carried, and there hung down a little closed claw. It was one of the bob-whites, with its beak hooked bitterly to show it was dead. "Now you go on home, Granny!"

"I bound to go to town, mister," said Phoenix. "The time come around."

He gave another laugh, filling the whole landscape. "I know you old colored people! Wouldn't miss going to town to see Santa Claus!"

But something held old Phoenix very still. The deep lines in her face went into a fierce and different radiation. Without warning, she had seen with her own eyes a flashing nickel fall out of the man's pocket onto the ground.

"How old are you, Granny?" he was saying.

"There is no telling, mister," she said, "no telling."

Then she gave a little cry and clapped her hands and said, "Git on away from here, dog! Look! Look at that dog!" She laughed as if in admiration. "He ain't scared of nobody. He a big black dog." She whispered, "Sic him!"

"Watch me get rid of that cur," said the man. "Sic him, Pete! Sic him!"

Phoenix heard the dogs fighting, and heard the man running and throwing sticks. She even heard a gunshot. But she was slowly bending forward by that time, further and further forward, the lids stretched down over her eyes, as if she were doing this in her sleep. Her chin was lowered almost to her knees. The yellow palm of her hand came out from the fold of her apron. Her fingers slid down and along the ground under the piece of money with the grace and care they would have in lifting an egg from under a setting hen. Then she slowly straightened up, she stood erect, and the nickel was in her apron pocket. A bird flew by. Her lips moved. "God watching me the whole time. I come to stealing."

The man came back, and his own dog panted about them. "Well, I scared him off that time," he said, and then he laughed and lifted his gun and pointed it at Phoenix.

She stood straight and faced him.

"Doesn't the gun scare you?" he said, still pointing it.

"No, sir, I seen plenty go off closer by, in my day, and for less than what I done," she said, holding utterly still.

He smiled, and shouldered the gun. "Well, Granny," he said, "you must be a hundred years old, and scared of nothing. I'd give you a dime if I had any money with me. But you take my advice and stay home, and nothing will happen to you."

"I bound to go on my way, mister," said Phoenix. She inclined her head in the red rag. Then they went in different directions, but she could hear the gun shooting again and again over the hill.

She walked on. The shadows hung from the oak trees to the road like curtains. Then she smelled wood-smoke, and smelled the river, and she saw a steeple and the cabins on their steep steps. Dozens of little black children whirled around her. There ahead was Natchez shining. Bells were ringing. She walked on.

In the paved city it was Christmas time. There were red and green electric lights strung and crisscrossed everywhere, and all turned on in the daytime. Old Phoenix would have been lost if she had not distrusted her eyesight and depended on her feet to know where to take her.

She paused quietly on the sidewalk where people were passing by. A lady came along in the crowd, carrying an armful of red-, green- and silver-wrapped presents; she gave off perfume like the red roses in hot summer, and Phoenix stopped her.

"Please, missy, will you lace up my shoe?" She held up her foot.

"What do you want, Grandma?"

"See my shoe," said Phoenix. "Do all right for out in the country, but wouldn't look right to go in a big building." "Stand still then, Grandma," said the lady. She put her packages down on the sidewalk beside her and laced and tied both shoes tightly.

"Can't lace 'em with a cane," said Phoenix. "Thank you, missy. I doesn't mind asking a nice lady to tie up my shoe, when I gets out on the street."

Moving slowly and from side to side, she went into the big building, and into a tower of steps, where she walked up and around and around until her feet knew to stop.

She entered a door, and there she saw nailed up on the wall the document that had been stamped with the gold seal and framed in the gold frame, which matched the dream that was hung up in her head.

"Here I be," she said. There was a fixed and ceremonial stiffness over her body.

"A charity case, I suppose," said an attendant who sat at the desk before her.

But Phoenix only looked above her head. There was sweat on her face, the wrinkles in her skin shone like a bright net.

"Speak up, Grandma," the woman said. "What's your name? We must have your history, you know. Have you been here before? What seems to be the trouble with you?"

Old Phoenix only gave a twitch to her face as if a fly were bothering her.

"Are you deaf?" cried the attendant.

But then the nurse came in.

"Oh, that's just old Aunt Phoenix," she said. "She doesn't come for herself — she has a little grandson. She makes these trips just as regular as clockwork. She lives away back off the Old Natchez Trace." She bent down. "Well, Aunt Phoenix, why don't you just take a seat? We won't keep you standing after your long trip." She pointed.

The old woman sat down, bolt upright in the chair.

"Now, how is the boy?" asked the nurse.

Old Phoenix did not speak.

"I said, how is the boy?"

But Phoenix only waited and stared straight ahead, her face very solemn and withdrawn into rigidity.

"Is his throat any better?" asked the nurse. "Aunt Phoenix, don't you hear me? Is your grandson's throat any better since the last time you came for the medicine?"

With her hands on her knees, the old woman waited, silent, erect and motionless, just as if she were in armor.

"You mustn't take up our time this way, Aunt Phoenix," the nurse said. "Tell us quickly about your grandson, and get it over. He isn't dead, is he?"

At last there came a flicker and then a flame of comprehension across her face, and she spoke.

"My grandson. It was my memory had left me. There I sat and forgot why I made my long trip."

"Forgot?" The nurse frowned. "After you came so far?"

Then Phoenix was like an old woman begging a dignified forgiveness for waking up frightened in the night. "I never did go to school, I was too old at the Surrender," she said in a soft voice. "I'm an old woman without an education. It was my memory fail me. My little grandson, he is just the same, and I forgot it in the coming."

"Throat never heals, does it?" said the nurse, speaking in a loud, sure voice to old Phoenix. By now she had a card with something written on it, a little list. "Yes. Swallowed lye. When was it? — January — two, three years ago — "

Phoenix spoke unasked now. "No, missy, he not dead, he just the same. Every little while his throat begin to close up again, and he not able to swallow. He not get his breath. He not able to help himself. So the time come around, and I go on another trip for the soothing medicine."

"All right. The doctor said as long as you came to get it, you could have it," said the nurse. "But it's an obstinate case."

"My little grandson, he sit up there in the house all wrapped up, waiting by himself," Phoenix went on. "We is the only two left in the world. He suffer and it don't seem to put him back at all. He got a sweet look. He going to last. He wear a little patch quilt and peep out holding his mouth open like a little bird. I remembers so plain now. I not going to forget him again, no, the whole enduring time. I could tell him from all the others in creation."

"All right." The nurse was trying to hush her now. She brought her a bottle of medicine. "Charity," she said, making a check mark in a book.

Old Phoenix held the bottle close to her eyes, and then carefully put it into her pocket.

"I thank you," she said.

"It's Christmas time, Grandma," said the attendant. "Could I give you a few pennies out of my purse?"

"Five pennies is a nickel," said Phoenix stiffly.

"Here's a nickel," said the attendant.

Phoenix rose carefully and held out her hand. She received the nickel and then fished the other nickel out of her pocket and laid it beside the new one. She stared at her palm closely, with her head on one side.

Then she gave a tap with her cane on the floor.

"This is what come to me to do," she said. "I going to the store and buy my child a little windmill they sells, made out of paper. He going to find it hard to

47

believe there such a thing in the world. I'll march myself back where he waiting, holding it straight up in this hand."

She lifted her free hand, gave a little nod, turned around, and walked out of the doctor's office. Then her slow step began on the stairs, going down.

Answer _true_ or _false_ for each of the following statements.

2.7 _____ The phoenix is a mythical bird of immortality that resurrects itself.

2.8 _____ Phoenix Jackson is a young white woman.

2.9 _____ Her journey takes place during December.

2.10 _____ Phoenix walks with a cane.

2.11 _____ Phoenix encounters several obstacles while walking along the path.

2.12 _____ A cat causes Phoenix to fall into the ditch.

2.13 _____ A black man lifts Phoenix out of the ditch.

2.14 _____ Phoenix tells the man that she is "bound to go to town."

2.15 _____ The man grossly underestimates the importance of Phoenix's mission and thinks that she wants to go to town to see Santa Claus.

2.16 _____ Phoenix calls attention to a stray cat so that she can pick up a nickel that dropped from the man's pocket.

2.17 _____ The city to which Phoenix travels is Natchez, Mississippi.

2.18 _____ A woman on the street ties Phoenix's shoes for her.

2.19 _____ The attendant in the doctor's office assumes that Phoenix is a regular paying patient.

2.20 _____ Phoenix makes the long journey along the path to get medicine for her grandson.

2.21 _____ Phoenix answers the nurse's questions about her grandson right away.

2.22 _____ When the nurse asks if her grandson is dead, Phoenix says, "yes."

2.23 _____ Phoenix says that she is going to buy her "child" a windmill.

John Updike (1932–2009). Often compared to William Dean Howells, John Updike focused upon the everyday life of the middle class. He was a precise and diligent craftsman who revealed the essence of life in America today. His stories diagnosed social and personal ills while offering a religious and moral cure.

Born in Reading, Pennsylvania, in 1932 and raised in the small town of Shillington, Updike was the only child of a high school mathematics teacher and a freelance writer. After graduating from Harvard in 1954, he attended Ruskin School of Drawing and Fine Art in Oxford, England. The following year, he returned to the United States to work as a reporter for *The New Yorker* magazine. Since that time, the magazine continued to publish his short stories, poems, and reviews.

In 1958 Updike published his first novel, *The Poorhouse Fair*. Exceedingly prolific, he published more than forty books, both nonfiction and fiction. His work won much critical and popular acclaim. *Rabbit is Rich* (1980) earned him the Pulitzer Prize for Fiction in 1982. And just nine years later, he won his second Pulitzer for *Rabbit at Rest* (1990). His collection of essays, *Hugging the Shore* (1983), won the National Book Critics Circle Award in 1983. Some of his short stories and novels have been reproduced on television and film.

Fill in each of the blanks using items from the following word list.

| cure | middle class | television |
| Pennsylvania | social | *The New Yorker* |

2.24   John Updike focused on the everyday life of the _____ .

2.25   His stories diagnose _____ and personal ills while offering a religious

and moral _____ .

2.26   Updike was raised in the small town of Shillington, _____ .

2.27   Updike worked as a reporter for _____ magazine.

2.28   Some of Updike's short stories and novels have been reproduced on _____

and film.

What to Look For:

John Updike's short stories and novels often depict the tragedies of contemporary American life. As Christians, we acknowledge that people are doomed to fail if they don't live according to God's law. As you read the following selection, notice how well the parents get along and how happy everyone seems. Yet, what is the reason they give for their separation? What does the father's "conscience" ask about the separation?

Separating

The day was fair. Brilliant. All that June the weather had mocked the Maples' internal misery with solid sunlight-golden shafts and cascades of green in which their conversations had wormed unseeing, their sad murmuring selves the only stain in Nature. Usually by this time of the year they had acquired tans; but when they met their elder daughter's plane on her return from a year in England they were almost as pale as she, though Judith was too dazzled by the sunny opulent jumble of her native land to notice. They did not spoil her homecoming by telling her immediately. Wait a few days, let her recover from jet lag, had been one of their formulations, in that string of gray dialogues — over coffee, over cocktails, over Cointreau — that had shaped the strategy of their dissolution, while the earth performed its annual stunt of renewal unnoticed beyond their closed windows. Richard had thought to leave at Easter; Joan had insisted they wait until the four children were at last assembled, with all exams passed and ceremonies attended, and the bauble of summer to console them. So he had drudged away, in love, in dread, repairing screens, getting the mowers sharpened, rolling and patching their new tennis court.

The court, clay, had come through its first winter pitted and windswept bare of redcoat. Years ago the Maples had observed how often, among their friends, divorce followed a dramatic home improvement, as if the marriage were making one last strong effort to live; their own worst crisis had come amid the plaster dust and exposed plumbing of a kitchen renovation. Yet, a summer ago, as canary-yellow bulldozers gaily churned a grassy, daisy-dotted knoll into a muddy plateau, and a crew of pigtailed young men raked and tamped clay into a plane, this transformation did not strike them as ominous, but festive in its impudence; their marriage could rend the earth for fun. The next spring, waking each day at dawn to a sliding sensation as if the bed were being tipped, Richard found the barren tennis court—its net and tapes still rolled in the barn—an environment congruous with his mood of purposeful desolation, and the crumbling of handfuls of clay into cracks and holes (dogs had frolicked on the court in a thaw; rivulets had evolved trenches) an activity suitably elemental and interminable. In his sealed heart he hoped the day would never come.

Now it was here. A Friday. Judith was reacclimated; all four children were assembled, before jobs and camps and visits again scattered them Joan thought they should be told one by one. Richard was for making an announcement at the table. She said, "I think just making an announcement is a cop-out. They'll start quarreling and playing to each other instead of focusing. They're each individuals, you know, not just some corporate obstacle to your freedom."

"O.K., O.K. I agree." Joan's plan was exact. That evening, they were giving Judith a belated welcome-home dinner, of lobster and champagne. Then, the party over, they, the two of them, who nineteen years before would push her in a baby carriage along Fifth Avenue to Washington Square, were to walk her out of the house, to the bridge across the salt creek, and tell her, swearing her to secrecy. Then Richard Jr., who was going directly from work to a rock concert in Boston, would be told, either late when he returned on the train or early Saturday morning before he went off to his job; he was seventeen and employed as one of a golf-course maintenance crew. Then the two younger children, John and Margaret, could, as the morning wore on, be informed.

"Mopped up, as it were," Richard said.

"Do you have any better plan? That leaves you the rest of Saturday to answer any questions, pack, and make your wonderful departure."

"No," he said, meaning he had no better plan, and agreed to hers, though to him it showed an edge of false order, a hidden plea for control, like Joan's long chore lists and financial accountings and, in the days when he first knew her, her too-copious lecture notes. Her plan turned one hurdle for him into four—four knife-sharp walls, each with a sheer blind drop on the other side.

All spring he had moved through a world of insides and outsides, of barriers and partitions. He and Joan stood as a thin barrier between the children and the truth. Each moment was a partition, with the past on one side and the future on the other, a future containing this unthinkable now. Beyond four knifelike walls a new life for him waited vaguely. His skull cupped a secret, a white face, a face both frightened and soothing, both strange and known, that he wanted to shield from tears, which he felt all about him, solid as the sunlight. So haunted, he had become obsessed with battening down the house against his absence, replacing screens and sash cords, hinges and latches—a Houdini making things snug before his escape.

The lock. He had still to replace a lock on one of the doors of the screened porch. The task, like most such, proved more difficult than he had imagined. The old lock, aluminum frozen by corrosion, had been deliberately rendered obsolete by manufacturers. Three hardware stores had nothing that even approximately matched the mortised hole its removal (surprisingly easy) left. Another hole had to be gouged, with bits too small and saws too big, and the old hole fitted with a block of wood—-the chisels dull, the saw rusty, his fingers thick with lack of sleep. The sun poured down, beyond the porch, on a world of neglect. The bushes already needed pruning, the windward side of the house was shedding flakes of paint, rain would get in when he was gone, insects, rot, death. His family, all those he would lose, filtered through the edges of his awareness as he struggled with screw holes, splinters, opaque instructions, minutiae of metal.

Judith sat on the porch, a princess returned from exile. She regaled them with stories of fuel shortages, of bomb scares in the Underground, of Pakistani workmen loudly lusting after her as she walked past on her way to dance school. Joan came and went, in and out of the house, calmer than she should have been, praising his struggles with the lock as if this were one more and not the last of their long chain of shared chores. The younger of his sons, John, now at fifteen suddenly, unwittingly handsome, for a few minutes held the rickety screen door while his father clumsily hammered and chiseled, each blow a kind of sob in Richard's ears. His younger daughter, having been at a slumber party, slept on the porch hammock through all the noise—heavy and pink, trusting and forsaken. Time, like the sunlight, continued relentlessly; the sunlight slowly slanted. Today was one of the longest days. The lock clicked, worked. He was through. He had a drink; he drank it on the porch, listening to his daughter. "It was so sweet," she was saying, "during the worst of it, how all the butchers and bakery shops kept open by candlelight. They're all so plucky and cute. From the papers, things sounded so much worse here—people shooting people in gas lines, and everybody freezing."

Richard asked her, "Do you still want to live in England forever?" Forever: the concept, now a reality upon him, pressed and scratched at the back of his throat.

"No," Judith confessed, turning her oval face to him, its eyes still childishly far apart, but the lips set as over something succulent and satisfactory. "I was anxious to come home. I'm an American." She was a woman. They had raised her; he and Joan had endured together to raise her, alone of the four. The others had still some raising left in them. Yet it was the thought of telling Judith—the image of her, their first baby, walking between them arm in arm to the bridge—that broke him. The partition between his face and the tears broke. Richard sat down to the celebratory meal with the back of his throat aching; the champagne, the lobster seemed phases of sunshine; he saw them and tasted them through tears. He blinked, swallowed, croakily joked about hay fever. The tears would not stop leaking through; they came not through a hole that could be plugged but through a permeable spot in a membrane, steadily, purely, endlessly, fruitfully. They became, his tears, a shield for himself against these others—their faces, the fact of their assembly, a last time as innocents, at a table where he sat the last time as head. Tears dropped from his nose as he broke the lobster's back; salt flavored his champagne as he sipped it; the raw clench at the back of his throat was delicious. He could not help himself.

His children tried to ignore his tears. Judith, on his right, lit a cigarette, gazed upward in the direction of her too energetic, too sophisticated exhalation; on her other side, John earnestly bent his face to the extraction of the last morsels—legs, tail segments—from the scarlet corpse. Joan, at the opposite end of the table, glanced at him surprised, her reproach displaced by a quick grimace, of forgiveness, or of salute to his superior gift of strategy. Between them, Margaret, no longer called Bean, thirteen and large for her age, gazed from the other side of his pane of tears as if into a shopwindow at something she coveted—at her father, a crystalline heap of splinters and memories. It was not she, however, but John who, in the kitchen, as they cleared the plates and carapaces away, asked Joan the question: *"Why is Daddy crying?"*

Richard heard the question but not the murmured answer. Then he heard Bean cry, "Oh, no — oh!" — the faintly dramatized exclamation of one who had long expected it.

51

John returned to the table carrying a bowl of salad. He nodded tersely at his father and his lips shaped the conspiratorial words "She told."

"Told what?" Richard asked aloud, insanely.

The boy sat down as if to rebuke his father's distraction with the example of his own good manners. He said quietly, "The separation."

Joan and Margaret returned; the child, in Richard's twisted vision, seemed diminished in size, and relieved, relieved to have had the bogieman at last proved real. He called out to her—the distances at the table had grown immense—"You knew, you always knew," but the clenching at the back of his throat prevented him from making sense of it. From afar he heard Joan talking, levelly, sensibly, reciting what they had prepared: it was a separation for the summer, an experiment. She and Daddy both agreed it would be good for them; they needed space and time to think; they liked each other but did not make each other happy enough, somehow.

Judith, imitating her mother's factual tone, but in her youth off-key, too cool, said, "I think it's silly. You should either live together or get divorced."

Richard's crying, like a wave that has crested and crashed, had become tumultuous; but it was overtopped by another tumult, for John, who had been so reserved, now grew larger and larger at the table. Perhaps his younger sister's being credited with knowing set him off. "Why didn't you *tell* us?" he asked, in a large round voice quite unlike his own. "You should have *told* us you weren't getting along."

Richard was startled into attempting to force words through his tears. "We do get along, that's the trouble, so it doesn't show even to us—" *That we do not love each other* was the rest of the sentence; he couldn't finish it.

Joan finished for him, in her style. "And we've always, *especially*, loved our children."

John was not mollified. "What do you care about *us*?" he boomed. "We're just little things you *had*." His sisters' laughing forced a laugh from him, which he turned hard and parodistic: "Ha ha *ha*." Richard and Joan realized simultaneously that the child was drunk, on Judith's homecoming champagne. Feeling bound to keep the center of the stage, John took a cigarette from Judith's pack, poked it into his mouth, let it hang from his lower lip, and squinted like a gangster.

"You're not little things we had," Richard called to him. "You're the whole point. But you're grown. Or almost."

The boy was lighting matches. Instead of holding them to his cigarette (for they had never seen him smoke; being "good" had been his way of setting himself apart), he held them to his mother's face, closer and closer, for her to blow out. Then he lit the whole folder—a hiss and then a torch, held against his mother's face. Prismed by his tears, the flame filled Richard's vision; he didn't know how it was extinguished. He heard Margaret say, "Oh stop showing off," and saw John, in response, break the cigarette in two and put the halves entirely into his mouth and chew, sticking out his tongue to display the shreds to his sister.

Joan talked to him, reasoning—a fountain of reason, unintelligible. "Talked about it for years...our children must help us...Daddy and I both want..." As the boy listened, he carefully wadded a paper napkin into the leaves of his salad, fashioned a ball of paper and lettuce, and popped it into his mouth, looking around the table for the expected laughter. None came. Judith said, "Be mature," and dismissed a plume of smoke.

Richard got up from this stifling table and led the boy outside. Though the house was in twilight, the outdoors still brimmed with light, the lovely waste light of high summer. Both laughing, he supervised John's spitting out the lettuce and paper and tobacco into the pachysandra. He took him by the hand—a square gritty hand, but for its softness a man's. Yet, it held on. They ran together up into the field, past the tennis court. The raw banking left by the bulldozers was dotted with daisies. Past the court and a flat stretch where they used to play family baseball stood a soft green rise glorious in the sun, each weed and species of grass distinct as illumination on parchment. "I'm sorry, so sorry," Richard cried. "You were the only one who ever tried to help me with all the jobs around this place."

Sobbing, safe within his tears and the champagne; John explained, "It's not just the separation, it's the whole crummy year, I *hate* that school, you can't make any friends, the history teacher's a scud."

They sat on the crest of the rise, shaking and warm from their tears but easier in their voices, and Richard tried to focus on the child's sad year—the weekdays long with homework, the weekends spent in his room with model airplanes, while his parents murmured down below, nursing their separation. How selfish, how blind, Richard thought; his eyes felt scoured. He told his son, "We'll think about getting you transferred. Life's too short to be miserable."

They had said what they could, but did not want the moment to heal, and talked on, about the school, about the tennis court, whether it would ever again be as good as it had been that first summer. They walked to inspect it and pressed a few more tapes more firmly down. A little stiltedly, perhaps trying now to make too much of the moment, Richard led the boy to the spot in the field where the view was best, of the metallic blue river, the emerald marsh, the scattered islands velvety with shadow in the low light, the white bits of beach far away. "See," he said. "It goes on being beautiful. It'll be here tomorrow."

"I know," John answered, impatiently. The moment had closed.

Back in the house, the others had opened some white wine, the champagne being drunk, and still sat at the table, the three females, gossiping. Where Joan sat had become the head. She turned, showing him a tearless face, and asked, "All right?"

"We're fine," he said, resenting it, though relieved, that the party went on without him.

In bed she explained, "I couldn't cry I guess because I cried so much all spring. It really wasn't fair. It's your idea, and you made it look as though I was kicking you out."

"I'm sorry," he said. "I couldn't stop. I wanted to but couldn't."

"You *didn't* want to. You loved it. You were having your way, making a general announcement."

"I love having it over," he admitted. "God, those kids were great. So brave and funny." John returned to the house, had settled to a model airplane his room, and kept shouting down to them, "I'm O.K. No sweat." "And the way," Richard went on, cozy in his relief, "they never questioned the reasons we gave. No thought of a third person. Not even Judith."

"That was touching," Joan said.

He gave her a hug. "You were great too. Very reassuring to everybody. Thank you." Guiltily, he realized he did not feel separated.

"You still have Dickie to do," she told him. These words set before him a black mountain in the darkness; its cold breath, its near weight affected his chest. Of the four children, his elder son was most like a conscience. Joan did not need to add, "That's one piece of your dirty work I won't do for you."

"I know. I'll do it. You go to sleep."

Within minutes, her breathing slowed, became oblivious and deep. It was quarter to midnight. Dickie's train from the concert would come in at one-fourteen. Richard set the alarm for one. He had slept atrociously for weeks. But whenever he closed his lids some glimpse of the last hours scorched them—Judith exhaling toward the ceiling in a kind of aversion, Bean's mute staring, the sun-struck growth of the field where he and John had rested. The mountain before him moved closer, moved within him; he was huge, momentous. The ache at the back of his throat felt stale. His wife slept as if slain beside him. When, exasperated by his hot lids, his crowded heart, he rose from bed and dressed, she awoke enough to turn over. He told her then, "Joan, if I could undo it all, I would."

"Where would you begin?" she asked. There was no place. Giving him courage, she was always giving him courage. He put on shoes without socks in the dark. The children were breathing in their rooms, the downstairs was hollow. In their confusion they had left lights burning. He turned off all but one, the kitchen overhead. The car started. He had hoped it wouldn't. He met only moonlight on the road; it seemed a diaphanous companion, flickering in the leaves along the roadside, haunting his rearview mirror like a pursuer, melting under his headlights. The center of town, not quite deserted, was eerie at this hour. A young cop in uniform kept company with a gang of T-shirted kids on the steps of the bank. Across from the railroad station, several bars kept open. Customers, mostly young, passed in and out of the warm night, savoring summer's novelty. Voices shouted from cars as they passed; an immense conversation seemed in progress. Richard parked and in his weariness put his head on the passenger seat, out of the commotion and wheeling lights. It was as when, in the movies, an assassin grimly carries his mission through the jostle of a carnival—except the movies cannot show the precipitous, palpable slope you cling to within. You cannot climb back down; you can only fall. The synthetic fabric of the car seat, warmed by his cheek, confided to him an ancient, distant scent of vanilla.

A train whistle caused him to lift his head. It was on time; he had hoped it would be late. The slender drawgates descended. The bell of approach tingled happily. The great metal body, horizontally fluted, rocked to a stop, and sleepy teen-agers disembarked, his son among them. Dickie did not show surprise that his father was meeting him at this terrible hour. He sauntered to the car with two friends, both taller than he. He said "Hi" to his father and took the passenger's seat with an exhausted promptness that expressed gratitude. The friends got into the back, and Richard was grateful; a few more minutes' postponement would be won by driving them home.

He asked, "How was the concert?"

"Groovy," one boy said from the back seat.

"It bit," the other said.

"It was O.K.," Dickie said, moderate by nature, so reasonable that in his childhood the unreason of the world had given him headaches, stomach aches, nausea. When the second friend had been dropped off at his dark house, the boy blurted, "Dad, my eyes are killing me with hay fever! I'm out there cutting that grass all day!"

"Do we still have those drops?"

"They didn't do any good last summer."

"They might this." Richard swung a U-turn on the empty street. The drive home took a few minutes. The mountain was here, in his throat. "Richard," he said, and felt the boy, slumped and rubbing his eyes, go tense at his tone, "I didn't come to meet you just to make your life easier. I came because your mother and I have some news for you, and you're a hard man to get ahold of these days. It's sad news."

"That's O.K." The reassurance came out soft, but quick, as if released from the tip of a spring.

Richard had feared that his tears would return and choke him, but the boy's manliness set an example, and his voice issued forth steady and dry. "It's sad news, but it needn't be tragic news, at least for you. It should have no practical effect on your life, though it's bound to have an emotional effect. You'll work at your job, and go back to school in September. Your mother and I are really proud of what you're making of your life; we don't want that to change at all."

"Yeah," the boy said lightly, on the intake of his breath, holding himself up. They turned the corner; the church they went to loomed like a gutted fort. The home of the woman Richard hoped to marry stood across the green. Her bedroom light burned.

"Your mother and I," he said, "have decided to separate. For the summer. Nothing legal, no divorce yet. We want to see how it feels. For some years now, we haven't been doing enough for each other, making each other as happy as we should be. Have you sensed that?"

"No," the boy said. It was an honest, unemotional answer: true or false in a quiz.

Glad for the factual basis, Richard pursued, even garrulously, the details. His apartment across town, his utter accessibility, the split vacation arrangements, the advantages to the children, the added mobility and variety of the summer. Dickie listened, absorbing. "Do the others know?"

"Yes."

"How did they take it?"

"The girls pretty calmly. John flipped out; he shouted and ate a cigarette and made a salad out of his napkin and told us how much he hated school."

His brother chuckled. "He did?"

"Yeah. The school issue was more upsetting for him than Mom and me. He seemed to feel better for having exploded."

"He did?" The repetition was the first sign that he was stunned.

"Yes. Dickie, I want to tell you something. This last hour, waiting for your train to get in, has been about the worst of my life. I hate this. *Hate* it. My father would have died before doing it to me." He felt immensely lighter, saying this. He had dumped the mountain on the boy. They were home. Moving swiftly as a shadow, Dickie was out of the car, through the bright kitchen. Richard called after him, "Want a glass of milk or anything?"

"No thanks."

"Want us to call the course tomorrow and say you're too sick to work?"

"No, that's all right." The answer was faint, delivered at the door to his room; Richard listened for the slam that went with a tantrum. The door closed normally, gently. The sound was sickening.

Joan had sunk into that first deep trough of sleep and was slow to awake. Richard had to repeat, "I told him."

"What did he say?"

"Nothing much. Could you go say goodnight to him? Please."

She left their room, without putting on a bathrobe. He sluggishly changed back into his pajamas and walked down the hall. Dickie was already in bed, Joan was sitting beside him, and the boy's bedside clock radio was murmuring music. When she stood, an inexplicable light—the moon?—outlined her body through the nightie. Richard sat on the warm place she had indented on the child's narrow mattress. He asked him, "Do you want the radio on like that?"

"It always is."

"Doesn't it keep you awake? It would me."

"No."

"Are you sleepy?"

"Yeah."

"Good. Sure you want to get up and go to work? You've had a big night."

"I want to."

Away at school this winter he had learned for the first time that you can go short of sleep and live. As an infant he had slept with an immobile, sweating intensity that had alarmed his babysitters. In adolescence he had often been the first of the four children to go to bed. Even now, he would go slack in the middle of a television show, his sprawled legs hairy and brown. "O.K. Good boy. Dickie, listen. I love you so much, I never knew how much until now. No matter how this works out, I'll always be with you. Really."

Richard bent to kiss an averted face but his son, sinewy, turned and with wet cheeks embraced him and gave him a kiss, on the lips, passionate as a woman's. In his father's ear he moaned one word, the crucial, intelligent word: "*Why?*"

Why. It was a whistle of wind in a crack, a knife thrust, a window thrown open on emptiness. The white face was gone, the darkness was featureless. Richard had forgotten why.

Answer *true* or *false* for each of the following statements.

2.29   _____   On the day that Judith returned from England, the weather was fair and brilliant.

2.30   _____   The parents decided to tell their children about the separation all at once at Easter.

2.31   _____   Because of the separation, Richard did not care about repairing things around the house.

2.32   _____   Joan tells the children that the separation was necessary because she and daddy were not making each other happy enough.

2.33   _____   Upon hearing the news of the separation Judith loses control and eats a cigarette and a napkin.

2.34   _____ Joan and Richard are so unhappy with each other that they refuse to share a bedroom.

2.35   _____ Dickie was most nearly Richard's conscience.

2.36   _____ As a child, the "unreason of the world" made Dickie sick.

2.37   _____ Richard tells Dickie as soon as possible about the separation.

2.38   _____ Noticing his parents' unhappiness, Dickie understands why his parents would want to separate.

2.39   _____ Dickie's only question about the separation is "Why?"

2.40   _____ Dickie's response to the separation makes Richard forget why they need a separation.

Robert Trail Spence Lowell, Jr. (1917–1977).

Robert Lowell's poetry is marked by public and personal change. A descendant of a long line of New England's elite, his great-granduncle was James Russell Lowell, the poet. As expected, he attended Harvard. But, desiring to distance himself from his New England past, he finished his education at Kenyon College in Ohio, graduating in 1940. It was the first in a series of rebellions against his family and structured society.

As a conscientious objector during World War II, he spent time in jail for his outspoken resistance to American policy and tactics. In 1947 he won the Pulitzer Prize for his collection of poems, *Lord Weary's Castle*. In the book, he expressed his new-found Catholicism and explored the history of his New England ancestors. Lowell had converted to Catholicism in 1940 but left it ten years later. In the 1950s, his poetry underwent a change. Abandoning the traditional forms, he approached poetry in a more autobiographical way, yet not without references to the changes in modern society.

During the 1960s, Lowell began to act as his own psychoanalyst, exploring his thoughts and experiences through his poetry. Because Lowell was involved in protesting the Vietnam War, many of his poems carry both political and personal impact. By the 1970s Lowell had been hospitalized several times for mental and emotional problems, divorced twice, and separated from his daughter. Consequently, his work became even more confessional. He became self-oriented, focusing on his feelings and troubles. Many critics do not care for his later work. Yet, in 1974 he won another Pulitzer Prize for his collection of sonnets, *The Dolphin*, which reflected a return to a more traditional form. Lowell's own moral and artistic downward spiral demonstrates well the disintegration of American society and culture.

 Underline the correct answer in each of the following statements.

2.41 Robert Lowell's poetry is marked by public and personal (consistency, change, evenness).

2.42 Robert Lowell was from a long line of (New England, Midwestern, Southern) elite.

2.43 Lowell left (Princeton, Duke, Harvard) to attend Kenyon College in Ohio.

2.44 In the 1950s, he began to abandon (modern, traditional, postmodern) form.

2.45 During the 1970s, Lowell's work began to be even more (traditional, politically oriented, confessional.)

What to Look For:

The "Epilogue" was the last piece of poetry in Lowell's final book, *Day by Day*. As you read it, pay attention to the speaker's attitude toward the role of an artist. How does he compare his work as a writer with that of a painter? According to Lowell, who gives the "poor passing facts" a "living name?"

Epilogue

Those blessed structures, plot and rhyme —
why are they no help to me now
I want to make
something imagined, not recalled?
I hear the noise of my own voice: 5
The painter's vision is not a lens,
it trembles to caress the light.
But sometimes everything I write
with the threadbare art of my eye
seems a snapshot,   10
lurid, rapid, garish, grouped,
heightened from life,
yet paralyzed by fact.
All's misalliance.
Yet why not say what happened?   15
Pray for the grace of accuracy
Vermeer* gave to the sun's illumination*
stealing like the tide across a map
to his girl solid with yearning.
We are poor passing facts   20
warned by that to give
each figure in the photograph
his living name.

by Robert Lowell, Copyright © Farrar, Straus and Giroux, LLC. Reprinted with permission

*Vermeer, Jan - Dutch painter (1632–75) known for his use of light
*sun's illumination - enlightened or deeper view of reality

Fill in each of the blanks using items from the following word list.

rhyme	facts	Vermeer's
lens	living	snapshot
plot	dissatisfied	

2.46   According to lines 1 and 2, the "blessed structures" of _____ and
_____ are limiting his imagination.

2.47   According to lines 5–7, the "noise of his own voice" tells him that painters paint more than
what they see through the _____ of their own eye.

2.48   Frustrated, the speaker says that his work is like a _____ , "paralyzed
by fact."

2.49   According to line 14, the speaker is _____ with his work.

2.50   According to lines 16–19, the speaker says to pray for _____ view of
reality.

2.51   According to lines 20, people are "poor passing _____ ."

2.52   According to lines 20–23, artists are warned to paint each figure with a

"_____ name."

 Review the material in this section in preparation for the Self-Test, which will check your mastery of both this particular section and your knowledge of the previous section.

SELF-TEST 2

Fill in each of the blanks using items from the following word list (each answer, 3 points).

traditional	God	valued
cure	lose	lens
plot	middle-class	truth
rhyme	social	television

2.01   In postmodern society, a universal standard of _____ no longer exists.

2.02   Novels and short stories of the postmodern era show elements of _____ works.

2.03   American culture has moved away from the deep truths of _____ .

2.04   Roethke _____ traditional forms of poetry.

2.05   Societies that stop believing in a universal standard of morals tend to _____ their ability to create great pieces of art.

2.06   John Updike focuses upon the everyday life of the _____ .

2.07   His stories diagnose _____ and personal ills while offering a religious and moral _____ .

2.08   Some of Updike's short stories and novels have been reproduced on _____ and film.

2.09   According to lines 1 and 2 of Lowell's "Epilogue," the "blessed structures" of _____ and _____ are limiting his imagination.

2.010   According to lines 5–7 of "Epilogue," the "noise of his own voice" tells him that painters paint more than what they see through the _____ of their own eye.

Answer *true* **or** *false* **for each of the following statements** (each answer, 2 points).

2.011   _____ In the short story, "The Displaced Person," Mrs. Shortley believed that Mr. Guizac was from the devil.

2.012   _____ Mrs. McIntyre believed that "Christ was just another D. P."

2.013   _____ The Guizacs are from a foreign country.

2.014   _____ In "A Worn Path," Phoenix Jackson is a young white woman.

2.015   _____ Phoenix encounters several obstacles while walking along the path.

2.016   _____ Phoenix calls attention to a stray cat so that she can pick up a nickel that dropped from a man's pocket.

2.017 _____ The attendant in the doctor's office assumes that Phoenix is a regular paying patient.

2.018 _____ Phoenix makes the long journey along the path to get medicine for her grandson.

2.019 _____ In Updike's short story "Separating," the parents decided to tell their children about the separation all at once at Easter.

2.020 _____ Because of the separation, Richard did not care about repairing things around the house.

2.021 _____ Joan tells the children that the separation was necessary because she and daddy were not making each other happy enough.

2.022 _____ Dickie was most nearly Richard's conscience.

2.023 _____ Dickie's only question about the separation is "Why?"

2.024 _____ Dickie's response to the separation makes Richard forget why they need a separation.

Underline the correct answer in each of the following statements (each answer, 2 points).

2.025 Eudora Welty has been described as "America's foremost living woman writer of (poetry, fiction, nonfiction)."

2.026 Welty's stories capture the details of life in the Deep (North, South, West).

2.027 Welty is a life-long resident of (Missouri, New York City, Mississippi).

2.028 The French Revolution exalted (human reason, divine revelation, the Bible).

2.029 The Modern Age searched for truth apart from (Christianity, communism, Marxism).

2.030 (Existentialism, Christianity, Marxism) is the belief that people have unlimited freedom of choice.

2.031 (God, Man, Government) alone is the author of truth.

2.032 Flannery O'Connor's stories paint a realistic picture of man's (sinfulness, purity, sinfulness).

2.033 The Iron Curtain limited the citizens of (democratic, communist, socialist) states from relations with Western Europe and the United States.

2.034 Robert Lowell's poetry is marked by public and personal (consistency, change, evenness).

2.035 Robert Lowell was from a long line of (New England, Midwestern, Southern) elite.

2.036 In the 1950s, Lowell began to abandon (modern, traditional, postmodern) form.

2.037 During the 1970s, Lowell's work began to be even more (traditional, politically oriented, confessional).

2.038 Frustrated, the speaker in "Epilogue" says that his work is like a (snapshot, portrait, landscape), "paralyzed by fact."

2.039 According to line 20 of "Epilogue," people are "poor passing (creatures, facts, beings)."

2.040 According to lines 20–23 of "Epilogue," artists are warned to paint each figure with a "(dying, crying, living) name."

For Thought and Discussion:

Explain to a parent/teacher John Updike's short story *Separating*. Be sure to mention the apparent happiness of the parents. In light of Jesus' provisions for divorce as stated in Matthew 19:8–9, discuss the validity of Richard and Joan's separation. Why is Dickie's question "Why?" so piercing to Richard's conscience? How is Richard and Joan's situation typical of many couples today?

77 / 96

Score _____

Teacher check _____

Initial   Date

III. SOCIAL ISSUES

Martin Luther King Jr. (1929–1968). Born into a long line of Baptist preachers, Martin Luther King Jr. understood the value and power of language. His speeches inspired many people, both black and white, to correct racial injustices nonviolently.

King was raised in a middle-class home in Atlanta where he was taught that people should not be judged by the color of their skin but by the content of their character. At the age of fifteen, he entered Morehouse College. Two years later, he was ordained a minister. King also studied at Crozer Theological Seminary and earned his Ph.D. degree in theology from Boston University. While doing postgraduate work, he became intently interested in the work of Mohandas K. Gandhi, who fought for social and political change in India. King adopted Gandhi's philosophy of nonviolent protest as his own.

In 1953 King married Coretta Scott and accepted the pastorate of a Baptist church in Montgomery, Alabama, the following year. After Rosa Parks was arrested for refusing to give up her bus seat to a white woman, King organized a bus boycott. The nonviolent protest lasted for a year, ending in the outlawing of segregation on buses in Montgomery. The victory pushed King to the forefront of the civil rights movement.

Despite threats on his life, his house being bombed, and unlawful arrests, King continued to carry out nonviolent protests. In August 1963, he led a march on Washington, during which he delivered his "I Have a Dream" speech to more than two hundred fifty thousand protestors. The following year, King was awarded the Nobel Peace Prize and the Civil Rights Act of 1964 was passed, desegregating hotels and restaurants. His dream was coming true.

But in 1968 the nation witnessed another nightmarish event. After delivering an address titled "I've Been to the Mountaintop," King was shot and killed while standing on a hotel balcony. In a most prophetic fashion, King had told the crowd that night, "I've seen the promised land. I may not get there with you. But I want you to know tonight, that we as a people will get to the promised land."

In many of his speeches, King used biblical stories to illustrate his people's struggles. He often compared himself with Moses and his people's difficulties with ancient Israel's enslavement to Egypt. This technique in literature is called typology. King's use of typology was powerful in its ability to persuade a nation to "let his people go!"

Fill in each of the blanks using items from the following word list.

Egypt	Baptist	protestors
segregation	Boston	Moses
boycott	Washington	Atlanta
Mohandas K. Gandhi	biblical	

3.1   Martin Luther King was raised in a middle-class home in _____ .

3.2   King was from a long line of _____ preachers.

3.3   King earned his Ph.D. degree in theology from _____ University.

3.4   He adopted the nonviolent protest philosophy of _____ .

3.5   He organized a year-long bus _____, which brought about the outlawing of bus _____ in Montgomery, Alabama.

3.6   In August 1963, he led the march on _____, in which he delivered his "I Have a Dream" speech to more than two hundred fifty thousand _____ .

3.7   King used _____ stories to illustrate his people's struggles.

3.8   He often compared himself with _____ and his people's difficulties with ancient Israel's enslavement to _____ .

What to Look For:

Dr. Martin Luther King's political speeches were firmly grounded in his training as a preacher. As you read the following address, notice the connections that he made between freedom and Christianity and between freedom and the Constitution of the United States. Why do you think Dr. King's speeches were so powerful?

Address at March on Washington for Jobs and Freedom

August 28, 1963
Washington, D. C.

"I Have a Dream"

I am happy to join with you today in what will go down in history as the greatest demonstration for freedom in the history of our nation.

Five score years ago, a great American, in whose symbolic shadow we stand today, signed the Emancipation Proclamation. This momentous decree came as a great beacon light of hope to millions of Negro slaves, who had been seared in the flames of withering injustice. It came as a joyous daybreak to end the long night of their captivity. But one hundred years later, the Negro still is not free. One hundred years later, the life of the Negro is still sadly crippled by the manacle of segregation and the chains of discrimination.

One hundred years later, the Negro lives on a lonely island of poverty in the midst of a vast ocean of material prosperity. One hundred years later, the Negro is still languished in the corners of American society and finds himself an exile in his own land. So we've come here today to dramatize a shameful condition.

In a sense we have come to our nation's capital to cash a check. When the architects of our republic wrote the magnificent words of the Constitution and the Declaration of Independence, they were signing a promissory note to which every American was to fall heir.

This note was a promise that all men, yes, black men as well as white men, would be guaranteed the inalienable rights of life, liberty and the pursuit of happiness.

It is obvious today that America has defaulted on this promissory note insofar as her citizens of color are concerned. Instead of honoring this sacred obligation, America has given the Negro people a bad check, a check which has come back marked "insufficient funds."

But we refuse to believe that the bank of justice is bankrupt. We refuse to believe that there are insufficient funds in the great vaults of opportunity of this nation. So we have come to cash this check, a check that will give us upon demand the riches of freedom and the security of justice.

We have also come to this hallowed spot to remind America of the fierce urgency of Now. This is no time to engage in the luxury of cooling off or to take the tranquilizing drug of gradualism. Now is the time to make real the promises of democracy. Now is the time to rise from the dark and desolate valley of segregation to the sunlit path of racial justice. Now is the time to lift our nation from the quicksands of racial injustice to the solid rock of brotherhood. Now is the time to make justice a reality for all of God's children.

It would be fatal for the nation to overlook the urgency of the moment. This sweltering summer of the Negro's legitimate discontent will not pass until there is an invigorating autumn of freedom and equality. Nineteen sixty-three is not an end but a beginning. Those who hope that the Negro needed to blow off steam and will now be content will have a rude awakening if the nation returns to business as usual.

There will be neither rest nor tranquility in America until the Negro is granted his citizenship rights. The whirlwinds of revolt will continue to shake the foundations of our nation until the bright day of justice emerges.

But there is something that I must say to my people who stand on the warm threshold which leads into the palace of justice. In the process of gaining our rightful place we must not be guilty of wrongful deeds.

Let us not seek to satisfy our thirst for freedom by drinking from the cup of bitterness and hatred. We must ever conduct our struggle on the high plane of dignity and discipline. We must not allow our creative protest to degenerate into physical violence. Again and again we must rise to the majestic heights of meeting physical force with soul force.

The marvelous new militancy which has engulfed the Negro community must not lead us to a distrust of all white people, for many of our white brothers, as evidenced by their presence here today, have come to realize that their destiny is tied up with our destiny. They have come to realize that their freedom is inextricably bound to our freedom. We cannot walk alone.

And as we walk, we must make the pledge that we shall always march ahead. We cannot turn back. There are those who are asking the devotees of civil rights, "When will you be satisfied?" We can never be satisfied as long as the Negro is the victim of the unspeakable horrors of police brutality.

We can never be satisfied as long as our bodies, heavy with the fatigue of travel, cannot gain lodging in the motels of the highways and the hotels of the cities. We cannot be satisfied as long as a Negro in Mississippi cannot vote and a Negro in New York believes he has nothing for which to vote.

No, no, we are not satisfied and we will not be satisfied until justice rolls down like waters and righteousness like a mighty stream.

I am not unmindful that some of you have come here out of great trials and tribulations. Some of you have come fresh from narrow jail cells. Some of you have come from areas where your quest for freedom left you battered by the storms of persecutions and staggered by the winds of police brutality. You have been the veterans of creative suffering. Continue to work with the faith that unearned suffering is redemptive.

Go back to Mississippi, go back to Alabama, go back to South Carolina, go back to Georgia, go back to Louisiana, go back to the slums and ghettos of our northern cities, knowing that somehow this situation can and will be changed.

Let us not wallow in the valley of despair. I say to you today, my friends, that even though we face the difficulties of today and tomorrow. I still have a dream.

It is a dream deeply rooted in the American dream.

I have a dream that one day this nation will rise up and live out the true meaning of its creed—we hold these truths to be self-evident that all men are created equal.

I have a dream that one day on the red hills of Georgia the sons of former slaves and the sons of former slave owners will be able to sit down together at the table of brotherhood.

I have a dream that one day even the state of Mississippi, a state sweltering with the heat of injustice, sweltering with the heat of oppression, will be transformed into an oasis of freedom and justice.

I have a dream that my four little children will one day live in a nation where they will not be judged by the color of their skin but by the content of their character.

I have a dream today!

I have a dream that one day, down in Alabama, with its vicious racists, with its governor having his lips dripping with the words of interposition and nullification; one day right down in Alabama little black boys and black girls will be able to join hands with little white boys and white girls as sisters and brothers.

I have a dream today!

I have a dream that one day every valley shall be exalted, and every hill and mountain shall be made low, the rough places will be made plain and the crooked places will be made straight and the glory of the Lord shall be revealed and all flesh shall see it together.

This is our hope. This is the faith that I will go back to the South with. With this faith we will be able to hew out of the mountain of despair a stone of hope. With this faith we will be able to transform the jangling discords of our nation into a beautiful symphony of brotherhood. With this faith we will be able to work together, to pray together, to struggle together, to go to jail together, to stand up for freedom together, knowing that we will be free one day. This will be the day, this will be the day when all of God's children will be able to sing with new meaning "My country 'tis of thee, sweet land of liberty, of thee I sing. Land where my fathers died, land of the Pilgrim's pride, from every mountainside, let freedom ring!" And if America is to be a great nation, this must become true.

And so let freedom ring from the prodigious hilltops of New Hampshire.

Let freedom ring from the mighty mountains of New York.

Let freedom ring from the heightening Alleghenies of Pennsylvania.

Let freedom ring from the snow-capped Rockies of Colorado.

Let freedom ring from the curvaceous slopes of California.

But not only that.

Let freedom ring from Stone Mountain of Georgia.

Let freedom ring from Lookout Mountain of Tennessee.

Let freedom ring from every hill and molehill of Mississippi, from every mountainside, let freedom ring!

And when this happens, when we allow freedom to ring, when we let it ring from every tenement and every hamlet, from every state and every city, we will

65

be able to speed up that day when all of God's children, black men and white men, Jews and Gentiles, Protestants and Catholics, will be able to join hands and sing in the words of the old Negro spiritual, "Free at last, free at last. Thank God Almighty, we are free at last."

by Martin Luther King, Copyright © Coretta Scott King

Answer *true* or *false* for each of the following statements.

3.9 _____ One hundred years after the Emancipation Proclamation, the Negro was still not free.

3.10 _____ The Constitution and the Declaration of Independence promised that only white men were guaranteed the unalienable rights of life, liberty, and the pursuit of happiness.

3.11 _____ There would be neither rest nor tranquility in America until the Negro was granted his citizenship rights.

3.12 _____ Protests must not be allowed to turn into physical violence.

3.13 _____ Whites had come to realize that their freedom was not tied to the freedom of blacks.

3.14 _____ Martin Luther King had a dream that one day the nation would live out the true meaning of its creed: "We hold these truths to be self-evident, that all men are created equal."

3.15 _____ He wished that one day children would not be judged by the color of their skin but by the content of their character.

3.16 _____ Our hope is in coming together to see the glory of the Lord revealed.

3.17 _____ Martin Luther King stressed the "beautiful symphony of brotherhood" among all Americans.

3.18 _____ For America to be a great nation, it must allow freedom to ring.

3.19 _____ Martin Luther King quotes two songs, a Negro spiritual and "America."

Ralph Ellison (1914–1994). Although deeply concerned about the struggles that faced black Americans, Ralph Ellison never wished to write "protest" works. He argued that he was "a human being, not just a black [writer]."

Born and raised in Oklahoma, Ellison attended Tuskegee Institute in Alabama. He began as a music major but moved to Harlem to earn more money for college as a jazz trumpet player. While in New York, he came in contact with Langston Hughes and Richard Wright, both of whom encouraged him to write.

From 1938 to 1942, he worked for the New York Federal Writers Project. Later, he joined the merchant marines. While on vacation, Ellison began work on his novel, *Invisible Man,* which took him seven years to complete. In 1952 it was published and became a bestseller. As one critic has observed, the story is about not only a black man who tries to find his identity in a cold and uncaring modern world but also all Americans and their search for self and being.

Invisible Man won Ellison the National Book Award and a number of lectureships, including at the University of Chicago and New York University. In 1964 he published a collection of essays titled *Shadow and Act.* His second novel, *Juneteenth,* was published posthumously in 1999.

Underline the correct answer in each of the following statements.

3.20   Ellison had proclaimed himself to be a (writer, speaker, lecturer) rather than a spokesman.

3.21   He was born and raised in (Texas, Arizona, Oklahoma).

3.22   He moved to (Atlanta, Harlem, Chicago) to earn more money for college as a jazz (flute, trumpet, drum) player.

3.23   (Louis Armstrong, Robert Lowell, Langston Hughes) encouraged him to write.

3.24   *Invisible Man* is about all (Asians, Africans, Americans) and their search for self and being.

3.25   Ellison was awarded (lectureships, scholarships, memberships) at the University of Chicago and New York University.

What to Look For:

Ralph Ellison's use of the stream-of-consciousness technique blurs the line between reality and illusion. As you read the following selection, notice what happens to the speaker when he loses touch with reality. Does he act responsibly? Does he become confused? How does he use his "invisibility" as an excuse to injure and steal?

Racial prejudice is a form of blindness. Because it judges people on the basis of their skin color, it fails to see the individual. Invisible Man *is a story of a black man's struggle to be known as an individual. He "loves light and desires light" because "The truth is the light and light is the truth." Light is a symbol of freedom. When people see him in the light of truth, then he will be an individual and not an invisible black man. However, everyone, no matter how they are treated, is accountable to God and society for their acts. His abusive use of a drug leads him into a dreamlike state that results only in confusion.*

Prologue
Prologue to Invisible Man by Ralph Ellison, Copyright © Random House, Inc. Reprinted with permission

I am an invisible man. No, I am not a spook like those who haunted Edgar Allan Poe; nor am I one of your Hollywood-movie ectoplasms. I am a man of substance, of flesh and bone, fiber and liquids—and I might even be said to possess a mind. I am invisible, understand, simply because people refuse to see me. Like the bodiless heads you see sometimes in circus sideshows, it is as though I have been surrounded by mirrors of hard, distorting glass. When they approach me they see only my surroundings, themselves, or figments of their imagination—indeed, everything and anything except me.

Nor is my invisibility exactly a matter of a biochemical accident to my epidermis. That invisibility to which I refer occurs because of a peculiar disposition of the eyes of those with whom I come in contact. A matter of the construction of their *inner* eyes, those eyes with which they look through their physical eyes upon reality. I am not complaining, nor am I protesting either. It is sometimes advantageous to be unseen, although it is most often rather wearing on the nerves. Then too, you're constantly being bumped against by those of poor vision. Or again, you often doubt if you really exist. You wonder whether you aren't simply a phantom in other people's minds. Say, a figure in a nightmare which the sleeper tries with all his strength to destroy. It's when you feel like this that, out of resentment, you begin to bump people back. And, let me confess, you feel that way most of the time. You ache with the need to convince yourself that you do exist in the real world, that you're a part of all the sound and anguish, and you strike out with your fists, you curse and you swear to make them recognize you. And, alas, it's seldom successful.

One night I accidentally bumped into a man, and perhaps because of the near darkness he saw me and called me an insulting name. I sprang at him, seized his coat lapels and demanded that he apologize. He was a tall blond man, and as my face came close to his he looked insolently out of his blue eyes and cursed me, his breath hot in my face as he struggled. I pulled his chin down sharp upon the crown of my head, butting him as I had seen the West Indians do, and I felt his flesh tear and the blood gush out, and I yelled, "Apologize! Apologize!" But he continued to curse and struggle, and I butted him again and again until he went down heavily, on his knees, profusely bleeding, I kicked him repeatedly, in a frenzy because he still uttered insults though his lips were frothy with blood. Oh yes, I kicked him! And in my outrage I got out my knife and prepared to slit his throat, right there beneath the lamplight in the deserted street, holding him in the collar with one hand, and opening the knife with my teeth—when it occurred to me that the man had not *seen* me, actually; that he, as far as he knew, was in the midst of a walking nightmare! And I stopped the blade, slicing the air as I pushed him away, letting him fall back to the street. I stared at him hard as the lights of a car stabbed through the darkness. He lay there, moaning on the asphalt; a man almost killed by a phantom. It unnerved me. I was both disgusted and ashamed. I was like a drunken man myself, wavering about on weakened legs. Then I was amused: Something in this man's thick head had sprung out and beaten him within an inch of his life. I began to laugh at this crazy discovery. Would he have awakened at the point of death? Would Death himself have freed him for wakeful living? But I didn't linger. I ran away into the dark, laughing so hard I feared I might rupture myself, The next day I saw his picture in the *Daily News,* beneath a caption stating that he had been "mugged." Poor fool, poor blind fool, I thought with sincere compassion, mugged by an invisible man!

Most of the time (although I do not choose as I once did to deny the violence of my days by ignoring it) I am not so overtly violent. I remember that I am invisible and walk softly so as not to awaken the sleeping ones. Sometimes it is best not to awaken them; there are few things in the world as dangerous as sleepwalkers. I learned in time though that it is possible to carry on a fight against them without their realizing it. For instance, I have been carrying on a fight with Monopolated Light & Power for some time now. I use their service and pay them nothing at all, and they don't know it. Oh, they suspect that power is being drained off, but they don't know where. All they know is that according to the master meter back there in their power station a [heck] of a lot of free current is disappearing somewhere, into the jungle of Harlem. The joke, of course, is that I don't live in Harlem but in a border area. Several years ago (before I discovered the advantages of being invisible) I went through the routine process of buying service and paying their outrageous rates. But no more. I gave up all that, along with my apartment, and my old way of life: That way based upon the fallacious assumption that I, like other men, was visible. Now, aware of my invisibility, I live rent-free in a building rented strictly to whites, in a section of the basement that was shut off and forgotten during the nineteenth century, which I discovered when I was trying to escape in the night from Ras the Destroyer. But that's getting too far ahead of the story, almost to the end, although the end is in the beginning and lies far ahead.

The point now is that I found a home—or a hole in the ground, as you will. Now don't jump to the conclusion that because I call my home a "hole" it is damp and cold like a grave; there are cold holes and warm holes. Mine is a warm hole. And remember, a bear retires to his hole for the winter and lives until spring; then he comes strolling out like the Easter chick breaking from its shell. I say all this to assure you that it is incorrect to assume that, because I'm invisible and live in a hole, I am dead. I am neither dead nor in a state of suspended animation. Call me Jack-the-Bear, for I am in a state of hibernation.

My hole is warm and full of light. Yes, *full* of light. I doubt if there is a brighter spot in all New York than this hole of mine, and I do not exclude Broadway. Or the Empire State Building on a photographer's dream night. But that is taking advantage of you. Those two spots are among the darkest of our whole civilization—pardon me, our whole culture (an important distinction, I've heard)—which might sound like a hoax, or a contradiction, but that (by contradiction, I mean) is how the world moves: Not like an arrow, but a boomerang. (Beware of those who speak of the *spiral* of history; they are preparing a boomerang. Keep a steel helmet handy.) I know; I have been boomeranged across my head so much that I now can see the darkness of lightness. And I love light. Perhaps you'll think it strange that an invisible man should need light, desire light, love light. But maybe it is exactly because I *am* invisible. Light confirms my reality, gives birth to my form. A beautiful girl once told me of a recurring nightmare in which she lay in the center of a large dark room and felt her face expand until it filled the whole room, becoming a formless mass while her eyes ran in bilious jelly up the chimney. And so it is with me. Without light I am not only invisible, but formless as well; and to be unaware of one's form is to live a death. I myself, after existing some twenty years, did not become alive until I discovered my invisibility.

That is why I fight my battle with Monopolated Light & Power. The deeper reason, I mean: It allows me to feel my vital aliveness. I also fight them for taking so much of my money before I learned to protect myself in my hole in the basement there are exactly 1,369 lights. I've wired the entire ceiling, every inch of it. And not with fluorescent bulbs, but with the older, more-expensive-to-operate kind, the filament type. An act of sabotage, you know. I've already begun to wire the wall. A junk man I know, a man of vision, has supplied me with wire and sockets. Nothing, storm or flood, must get in the way of our need for light and ever more and brighter light. The truth is the light and light is the truth. When I finish all four walls, then I'll start on the floor. just how that will go, I don't know. Yet when you have lived invisible as long as I have you develop a certain ingenuity. I'll solve the problem. And maybe I'll invent a gadget to place my coffee pot on the fire while I lie in bed, and even invent a gadget to warm my bed—like the fellow I saw in one of the picture magazines who made himself a gadget to warm his shoes! Though invisible, I am in the great American tradition of tinkers. That makes me kin to Ford, Edison and Franklin. Call me, since I have a theory and a concept, a "thinker-tinker." Yes, I'll warm my shoes; they need it, they're usually full of holes. I'll do that and more.

Now I have one radio-phonograph; I plan to have five. There is a certain acoustical deadness in my hole, and when I have music I want to *feel* its vibration, not only with my ear but with my whole body. I'd like to hear five recordings of Louis Armstrong playing and singing "What Did I Do to Be so Black and Blue"—all at the same time. Sometimes now I listen to Louis while I have my favorite dessert of vanilla ice cream and sloe gin. I pour the red liquid over the white mound, watching it glisten and the vapor rising as Louis bends that military instrument into a beam of lyrical sound. Perhaps I like Louis Armstrong because he's made poetry out of being invisible. I think it must be because he's unaware that he is invisible. And my own grasp of invisibility aids me to understand his music. Once when I asked for a cigarette, some jokers gave me a reefer, which I lighted when I got home and sat listening to my phonograph. It was a strange evening. Invisibility, let me explain, gives one a slightly different sense of time, you're never quite on the beat. Sometimes you're ahead and sometimes behind.

Instead of the swift and imperceptible flowing of time, you are aware of its nodes, those points where time stands still or from which it leaps ahead. And you slip into the breaks and look around. That's what you hear vaguely in Louis' music.

Once I saw a prizefighter boxing a yokel. The fighter was swift and amazingly scientific. His body was one violent flow of rapid rhythmic action. He hit the yokel a hundred times while the yokel held up his arms in stunned surprise. But suddenly the yokel, rolling about in the gale of boxing gloves, struck one blow and knocked science, speed and footwork as cold as a well-digger's posterior. The smart money hit the canvas. The long shot got the nod. The yokel had simply stepped inside of his opponent's sense of time. So under the spell of the reefer I discovered a new analytical way of listening to musk. The unheard sounds came through, and each melodic line existed of itself, stood out clearly from all the rest, said its piece, and waited patiently for the other voices to speak. That night I found myself hearing not only in time, but in space as well. I not only entered the music but descended, like Dante, into its depths.

And *beneath the swiftness of the hot tempo there was a slower tempo and a cave and I entered it and looked around and heard an old woman singing a spiritual as full of Weltschmerz as flamenco, and beneath that lay a still lower level on which I saw a beautiful girl the color of ivory pleading in a voice like my mothers as she stood before a group of slaveowners who bid for her naked body, and below that I found a lower level and a more rapid tempo and I heard someone shout:*

"Brothers and sisters, my text this morning is the 'Blackness of Blackness.'"

And a congregation of voices answered: "That blackness is most black, brother, most black..."

"In the beginning..."

"At the very start, " they cried.

"...there was blackness..."

"Preach it..."

"...and the sun..."

"The sun, Lawd..."

"...was bloody red..."

"Red..."

"Now black is..." the preacber shouted.

"Bloody..."

"I said black is..."

"Preach it, brother..."

"...an' black ain't..."

"Red, Lawd, red. He said it's red!"

"Amen, brother..."

"Black will git you..."

"Yes, it will..."

"Yes, it will..."

"...an' black won't"

"Naw, it won't!"

"It do..."

"It do, Lawd..."

"...an' it don't."

"Halleluiah..."

"...It'll put you, glory, glory, Oh my Lawd, in the WHALE'S BELLY."

"Preach it, dear brother..."

"...an' make you tempt..."

"Good God a-migbty!"

"Old Aunt Nelly!"

"Black will make you..."

"Black..."

"...or black will un-make you."

"Ain't it the truth, Lawd?"

And at that point a voice of trombone timbre screamed at me, "Git out of here, you fool! Is you ready to commit treason?"

And I tore myself away, hearing the old singer of spirituals moaning, "Go curse your God, boy, and die."

I stopped and questioned her, asked her what was wrong.

"I dearly loved my master, son," she said.

"You should have hated him," I said.

"He gave me several sons," she said, "and because I loved my sons I learned to love their father though I hated him too."

"I too have become acquainted with ambivalence, "I said. "That's why I'm here."

"What's that?"

"Nothing, a word that doesn't explain it. Wby do you moan?"

"I moan this way 'cause he's dead," she said.

"Then tell me, who is that laughing upstairs?"

"Them's my sons. They glad."

"Yes, I can understand that too, "I said.'I laughs too, but I moans too. He promised to set us free but be never could bring hisself to do it. Still I loved him..."

"Loved him? You mean...?"

"Oh yes, but I loved something else even more."

"Wbat more?"

"Freedom."

"Freedom," I said. "Maybe freedom lies in hating."

"Naw, son, it's in loving. I loved him and give him the poison and be withered away like a frost-bit apple. Them boys woulda tore him to pieces with they home-made knives."

71

"A mistake was made somewbere," I said, "I'm confused."

And I wished to say other things, but the laughter upstairs became too loud and moan-like for me and I tried to break out of it, but I couldn't. Just as I was leaving I felt an urgent desire to ask her what freedom was and went back. She sat with her head in her hands, moaning softly; ber leather-brown face was filled witb sadness.

"Old woman, what is this freedom you love so well?" I asked around a corner of my mind.

She looked surprised, then thoughtful, then baffled. 'I done forgot, son. It's all mixed up. First I think it's one thing, then I think it's another. It gits my head to spinning. I guess now it ain't nothing but knowing how to say what I got up in my head. But it's a hard job, son. Too much is done happen to me in too short a time. Hit's like I have a fever ever' time I starts to walk my head gits to swirling and I falls down. Or if it ain't that, it's the boys; they gits to laughing and wants to kill up the whitefolks. They's bitter, that's what they is...'

"'But what about freedom?"

"Leave me 'lone, boy; my head aches!"

I left her, feeling dizzy myself I didn't get far.

Suddenly one of the sons, a big fellow six feet tall, appeared out of nowhere and struck me with his fist.

"What's the matter, man?" I cried.

"You made Ma cry!"

"But how?" I said, dodging a blow.

"Askin' her them questions, that's how. Git outa here and stay, and next time you got questions like that, ask yourself!"

He held me in a grip like cold stone, his fingers fastening upon my windpipe until I thought I would suffocate before he finally allowed me to go. I stumbled about dazed, the music beating hysterically in my ears. It was dark. My head cleared and I wandered down a dark narrow passage, thinking I heard his footsteps hurrying behind me. I was sore, and into my being had come a profound craving for tranquillity, for peace and quiet, a state I felt I could never achieve. For one thing, the trumpet was blaring and the rhythm was too hectic. A tom-tom beating like heart-thuds began drowning out the trumpet, filling my ears. I longed for water and I heard it rushing through the cold mains my fingers touched as I felt my way, but I couldn't stop to search because of tbe footsteps behind me.

"Hey, Ras, " I called "Is it you, Destroyer? Rinehart?"

No answer, only the rhythmic footsteps behind me. Once I tried crossing the road, but a speeding machine struck me, scraping the skin from my leg as it roared past.

Then somehow I came out of it, ascending hastily from this underworld of sound to hear Louis Armstrong innocently asking,

What did I do

To be so black

And blue?

At first I was afraid; this familiar music had demanded action, the kind of which I was incapable, and yet had I lingered there beneath the surface I might have attempted to act. Nevertheless, I know now that few really listen to this music, I sat on the chair's edge in a soaking sweat, as though each of my 1,369 bulbs had every one become a klieg light in an individual setting for a third degree with Ras and Rinehart in charge. It was exhausting—as though I had held my breath continuously for an hour under the terrifying serenity that comes from days of intense hunger. And yet, it was a strangely satisfying experience for an invisible man to hear the silence of sound. I had discovered unrecognized compulsions of my being—even though I could not answer "yes" to their promptings. I haven't smoked a reefer since, however; not because they're illegal, but because to *see* around corners is enough (that is not unusual when you are invisible). But to hear around them is too much; it inhibits action. And despite Brother Jack and all that sad, lost period of the Brotherhood, I believe in nothing if not in action.

Please, a definition: A hibernation is a covert preparation for a more overt action.

Besides, the drug destroys one's sense of time completely. If that happened, I might forget to dodge some bright morning and some cluck would run me down with an orange and yellow street car, or a bilious bus! Or I might forget to leave my hole when the moment for action presents itself.

Meanwhile I enjoy my life with the compliments of Monopolated Light & Power. Since you never recognize me even when in closest contact with me, and since, no doubt, you'll hardly believe that I exist, it won't matter if you know that I tapped a power line leading into the building and ran it into my hole in the ground. Before that I lived in the darkness into which I was chased, but now I see. I've illuminated the blackness of my invisibility—and vice versa. And so I play the invisible music of my isolation. The last statement doesn't seem just right, does it? But it is; you hear this music simply because music is heard and seldom seen, except by musicians. Could this compulsion to put invisibility down in black and white be thus an urge to make music of invisibility? But I am an orator, a rabble rouser—Am? I *was,* and perhaps shall be again, Who knows? All sickness is not unto death, neither is invisibility.

I can hear you say, "What a horrible, irresponsible [clod]!" And you're right. I leap to agree with you. I am one of the most irresponsible beings that ever lived. Irresponsibility is part of my invisibility; any way you face it, it is a denial. But to whom can I be responsible, and why should I be, when you refuse to see me? And wait until I reveal how truly irresponsible I am. Responsibility rests upon recognition, and recognition is a form of agreement. Take the man whom I almost killed: Who was responsible for that near murder—I? I don't think so, and I refuse it. I won't buy it. You can't give it to me. *He* bumped *me, he* insulted *me.* Shouldn't he, for his own personal safety, have recognized my hysteria, my "danger potential?" He, let us say, was lost in a dream world. But didn't *he* control that dream world-which, alas, is only too real—and didn't *he* rule me out of it? And if he had yelled for a policeman, wouldn't I have been taken for the offending one? Yes, yes, yes! Let me agree with you, I was the irresponsible one; for I should have used my knife to protect the higher interests of society. Some day that kind of foolishness will cause us tragic trouble. All dreamers and sleepwalkers must pay the price, and even the invisible victim is responsible for the fate of all. But I shirked that responsibility; I became too snarled in the incompatible notions that buzzed within my brain. I was a coward...

But what did I do to be so blue? Bear with me.

Answer *true* or *false* for each of the following statements.

3.26 _____ The speaker says that he is an invisible man because people refuse to see him.

3.27 _____ His invisibility is a construction of people's *inner* eyes, not their physical eyes.

3.28 _____ The invisible man nearly kills a "blonde man" for seeing him.

3.29 _____ The invisible man calls his home a "palace in the sky."

3.30 _____ Light symbolizes bondage.

3.31 _____ Light confirms and gives form to the invisible man's reality.

3.32 _____ The invisible man fights his battle with Monopolated Light & Power.

3.33 _____ The invisible man likes the music of Louis Armstrong because he made poetry out of being visible.

3.34 _____ The use of reefer causes the invisible man to slip into a state of illusion.

3.35 _____ The preacher's text is the "Whiteness of Whiteness."

3.36 _____ The old woman and the invisible man become confused over what is freedom.

3.37 _____ When the invisible man comes out of his illusionary state, he hears Louis Armstrong asking, "What did I do to be so black and blue?"

3.38 _____ The invisible man refuses to take responsibility for the near murder.

3.39 _____ He claims that the blonde man's foolishness — blindness — will one day cause tragic trouble.

Gwendolyn Brooks (1917–2000). She was born in Topeka, Kansas, but reared in Chicago. The city and its black society are the subject matter of much of her poetry. At an early age, Brooks demonstrated a talent for writing. Before she was twenty, she was published regularly in the *Chicago Defender*. But it wasn't until Brooks was married and a mother that she published her first book of poetry, *A Street in Bronzeville* (1945). Just five years later, she won the Pulitzer Prize for Poetry with *Annie Allen* (1949), her second book of poetry.

The history of Gwendolyn Brooks's work traces the progression of black art and culture in America. Before the 1960s, her work was traditional and intended for both white and black readers. One critic has noted that after 1967, when she "rediscovered her blackness," her work began to reflect more and more a push toward black community and pride. Her poetry is filled with rhythms of black culture and society—street talk, spirituals, the blues and jazz—yet much of it is written in traditional form.

Fill in each of the blanks using items from the following word list.

traditional	Chicago	pride
community	poetry	black

3.40   Gwendolyn Brooks was raised in _____ .

3.41   Chicago and its black society are the subject matter of much of her _____ .

3.42   The history of her work traces the progression of _____ art and culture
        in America.

3.43   Her most recent work reflects a push toward black _____ and
        _____ .

3.44   Much of her poetry is written in _____ form.

What to Look For:

Gwendolyn Brooks recorded in her poetry the struggles and pains of life in the ghettos. Like many other social critics, she uses sarcasm to convey her message. As you read the following selection, notice the speaker's attitude toward the women from the "Ladies' Betterment League." Do you think that the ladies truly want to help the poor? In what ways do the ladies "love" the poor? Is the speaker's use of "loathe-love" sarcastic?

The Lovers of the Poor

arrive. The Ladies from the Ladies' Betterment League

Arrive in the afternoon, the late light slanting

In diluted gold bars across the boulevard brag

Of proud, seamed faces with mercy and murder hinting

Here, there, interrupting, all deep and debonair,

The pink paint on the innocence of fear;

Walk in a gingerly manner up the hall.

Cutting with knives served by their softest care,

Served by their love, so barbarously fair.

Whose mothers taught: You'd better not be cruel!

You had better not throw stones upon the wrens!

Herein they kiss and coddle and assault

Anew and dearly in the innocence

With which they baffle nature. Who are full,

Sleek, tender-clad, fit, fiftyish, a-glow, all

Sweetly abortive, hinting at fat fruit,

Judge it high time that fiftyish fingers felt

Beneath the lovelier planes of enterprise.

To resurrect. To moisten with milky chill.

To be a random hitching-post or plush.

To be, for wet eyes, random and handy hem.

        Their guild is giving money to the poor.

The worthy poor. The very very worthy

And beautiful poor. Perhaps just not too swarthy?

Perhaps just not too dirty nor too dim

Nor—passionate. In truth, what they could wish

Is—something less than derelict or dull.

Not staunch enough to stab, though, gaze for gaze!

God shield them sharply from the beggar-bold!

The noxious needy ones whose battle's bald

Nonetheless for being voiceless, hits one down.

        But it's all so bad! and entirely too much for them.

The stench; the urine, cabbage, and dead beans,

Dead porridges of assorted dusty grains,

The old smoke, *heavy* diapers, and, they're told,

Something called chitterlings. The darkness. Drawn

Darkness, or dirty light. The soil that stirs.

The soil that looks the soil of centuries.

And for that matter the general oldness. Old

Wood. Old marble. Old tile. Old old old.

Not homekind Oldness! Not Lake Forest, Glencoe.

Nothing is sturdy, nothing is majestic,

There is no quiet drama, no rubbed glaze, no

Unkillable infirmity of such

A tasteful turn as lately they have left,

Glencoe, Lake Forest, and to which their cars

Must presently restore them. When they're done

With dullards and distortions of this fistic

Patience of the poor and put-upon.

        They've never seen such a make-do-ness as

Newspaper rugs before! In this, this "flat,"

Their hostess is gathering up the oozed, the rich

Rugs of the morning (tattered, the bespattered...)

Readies to spread clean rugs for afternoon.

Here is a scene for you. The Ladies look,

In horror, behind a substantial citizeness

Whose trains clank out across her swollen heart.

Who, arms akimbo, almost fills a door.

All tumbling children, quilts dragged to the floor

And tortured thereover, potato peelings, soft-

Eyed kitten, hunched-up, haggard, to-be-hurt.

   Their League is allotting largesse to the Lost.

But to put their clean, their pretty money, to put

Their money collected from delicate rose-fingers

Tipped with their hundred flawless rose-nails seems...

   They own Spode, Lowestoft, candelabra,

Mantels, and hostess gowns, and sunburst clocks,

Turtle soup, Chippendale, red satin "hangings,"

Aubussons and Hattie Carnegie. They Winter

In Palm Beach, cross the Water in June; attend,

When suitable, the nice Art Institute;

Buy the right books in the best bindings; saunter

On Michigan, Easter mornings, in sun or wind.

Oh Squalor! This sick four-story hulk, this fibre

With fissures everywhere! Why, what are bringings

Of loathe-love largesse? What shall peril hungers

So old old, what shall flatter the desolate?

Tin can, blocked fire escape and chitterling

And swaggering seeking youth and the puzzled wreckage

Of the middle passage, and urine and stale shames

And, again, the porridges of the underslung

And children children children. Heavens! That

Was a rat, surely, off there, in the shadows? Long

And long-tailed? Gray? The Ladies from the Ladies'

Betterment League agree it will be better

To achieve the outer air that rights and steadies,

To hie to a house that does not holler, to ring

Bells elsetime, better presently to cater

To no more Possibilities, to get

Away. Perhaps the money can be posted.

Perhaps they two may choose another Slum!

Some serious sooty half-unhappy home! —

Where loathe-love likelier may be invested.

Keeping their scented bodies in the center

Of the hall as they walk down the hysterical hall,

They allow their lovely skirts to graze no wall,

Are off at what they manage of a canter,

And, resuming all the clues of what they were,

Try to avoid inhaling the laden air.

Lake Forest, Glencoe - a wealthy suburb of Chicago

➤→   **Answer** *true* or *false* **for each of the following statements.**

3.45   _____   According to line 4, the ladies have proud faces.

3.46   _____   According to line 9, the ladies' "love" is gentle and genuine.

3.47   _____   The ladies are about twenty years old.

3.48   _____   According to lines 19–23, the guild is giving money "to resurrect" the poor.

3.49   _____   The ladies only want to give to anyone who needs it.

3.50   _____   According to lines 33–41, the ghetto is nothing like the prosperous suburb of Chicago from which the ladies come.

3.51   _____   In the ghetto, "everything is sturdy, everything is majestic."

3.52   _____   According to lines 91–93, the ladies refuse to give their "loathe-love" because there is no hope of change.

3.53   _____   According to lines 94–99, the ladies were so disgusted that they tried to avoid coming in contact with anything.

Before you take this last Self-Test, you might want to do one or more of the following self-checks.

1.   _____   Read the objectives. Determine if you can do them.

2.   _____   Restudy the material related to any objectives that you cannot do.

3.   _____   Use the **SQ3R** study procedure to review the material:

a. Scan the sections.
b. **Q**uestion yourself again (review the questions you wrote initially).
c. **R**ead to answer your questions.
d. **R**ecite the answers to yourself.
e. **R**eview areas you didn't understand.

4.   _____   Review all vocabulary, activities, and Self-Tests, writing a correct answer for each wrong answer you originally chose.

SELF-TEST 3

Fill in each of the blanks using items from the following word list (each answer, 2 points).

Baptist	black	Washington
community	Egypt	valued
lose	middle-class	truth
Mohandas K. Gandhi	Moses	traditional
poetry	social	pride
protestors		

3.01   In postmodern society, a universal standard of _____ no longer exists.

3.02   Societies that stop believing in a universal standard of morals tend to _____ their ability to create great pieces of art.

3.03   Roethke _____ traditional forms of poetry.

3.04   John Updike focuses upon the everyday life of the _____ .

3.05   Updike's stories diagnose _____ and personal ills while offering a religious and moral cure.

3.06   King was from a long line of _____ preachers.

3.07   He adopted the nonviolent protest philosophy of _____ .

3.08   In August 1963, King led the March on _____ , in which he delivered his "I Have a Dream" speech to more than two hundred fifty thousand _____ .

3.09   He often compared himself to _____ and his people's difficulties to ancient Israel's enslavement to _____ .

3.010   Chicago and its black society are the subject matter of much of Gwendolyn Brooks' _____ .

3.011   The history of Brooks's work traces the progression of _____ art and culture in America.

3.012   Her most recent work reflects a push toward black _____ and _____ .

3.013   Much of her poetry is written in _____ form.

Answer *true* or *false* for each of the following statements (each answer, 2 points).

3.014   _____   In the short story, "The Displaced Person," Mrs. Shortley believed that Mr. Guizac was from the devil.

3.015   _____   Mrs. McIntyre believed that "Christ was just another D. P."

3.016   _____   In Updike's short story "Separating," Dickie was most nearly Richard's conscience.

3.017   _____   Martin Luther King Jr. had a dream that one day the nation would live out the true meaning of its creed: "We hold these truths to be self-evident, that all men are created equal."

3.018   _____   Martin Luther King Jr. wished that one day children would not be judged by the color of their skin but by the content of their character.

3.019 _____ Martin Luther King stressed the "beautiful symphony of brotherhood" among all Americans.

3.020 _____ Martin Luther King quoted two songs in his "I Have a Dream" speech: a Negro spiritual and "America."

3.021 _____ In Ellison's book *Invisible Man,* the speaker says that he is an invisible man because people refuse to see him.

3.022 _____ Light confirms and gives form to the invisible man's reality.

3.023 _____ The invisible man likes the music of Louis Armstrong because he made poetry out of being visible.

3.024 _____ The old woman and the invisible man become confused over what is freedom.

3.025 _____ When the invisible man comes out of his illusionary state, he hears Louis Armstrong asking, "What did I do to be so black and blue?"

3.026 _____ The invisible man refuses to take responsibility for the near murder.

3.027 _____ According to line 5 of Brooks's poem "Lovers of the Poor," the ladies have proud faces.

3.028 _____ The ladies only want to give to anyone who needs it.

3.029 _____ According to lines 34–42, the ghetto is nothing like the prosperous suburb of Chicago from which the ladies come.

3.030 _____ According to lines 90–92, the ladies refuse to give their "loathe-love" because there is no hope of change.

Underline the correct answer in each of the following statements (each answer, 4 points).

3.031 The Modern Age searched for truth apart from (Christianity, communism, Marxism).

3.032 Robert Lowell's poetry is marked by public and personal (consistency, change, evenness).

3.033 Flannery O'Connor's stories paint a realistic picture of man's (purity, sinfulness, happiness).

3.034 Ellison has proclaimed himself to be a (writer, speaker, lecturer) rather than a spokesman.

3.035 He moved to (Atlanta, Harlem, Chicago) to earn more money for college as a jazz (flute, trumpet, drum) player.

3.036 (Louis Armstrong, Robert Lowell, Langston Hughes) encouraged him to write.

3.037 The Invisible Man is about all (Asians, Africans, Americans) and their search for self and being.